P9-EJU-981

HOUNDED

HOUNDED

The Lowdown on Life from Three Dachshunds

A MEMOIR

MATT ZISELMAN

CENTER STREET

New York   Boston   Nashville

Center Street
Hachette Book Group
237 Park Avenue
New York, NY 10017

CenterStreet.com

Printed in the United States of America

RRD-C

First Edition: May 2013
10 9 8 7 6 5 4 3 2 1

Center Street is a division of Hachette Book Group, Inc.
The Center Street name and logo are trademarks of Hachette Book Group, Inc.

The Hachette Speakers Bureau provides a wide range of authors for speaking events. To find out more, go to www.HachetteSpeakersBureau.com or call (866) 376-6591.

The publisher is not responsible for websites (or their content) that are not owned by the publisher.

Library of Congress Control Number: 2013930542

This book is dedicated to my mom and dad for giving me life.

And to Melissa and Emily who *are* my life.

Acknowledgments

While it's often been said that writing a book is a lonely business, bringing a book to fruition is anything *but* lonely, usually involving a slew of talented, dedicated people. That's certainly the case with *Hounded*. And while I don't think the people below actually qualify as an official slew, I would be remiss if I didn't thank them for their contributions—both large and small—in helping to bring *Hounded* to life.

Wendy Sherman for ably steering me through the sometimes-scary publishing waters, and for believing, from the very beginning, that *Hounded* was more than just a "dog" book.

Kate Hartson. Before *Hounded* was even fully realized, I knew that it would take a special person to "get it." I'm so glad that special person turned out to be you. Thank you for your guidance, patience, and commitment to ensuring that *Hounded* be the best it could possibly be.

Lauren Rohrig for answering every question with a smile.

Jody Waldrup, Art Director and Dachshund wrangler extraordinaire, thank you for a cover that makes me smile every time I see it.

To everyone at Center Street and Hachette my deepest gratitude for your unwavering support, unbridled enthusiasm

Acknowledgments

and Herculean efforts. You've made this first timer feel very much at home.

Herman Estevez for photographs that make words seem redundant.

Dr. Sharon at Barnside Veterinary Hospital for taking such good care of Baxter, Maya and Molly and—*I promise*—we're going to cut back on the treats.

Wade Rouse and Gary Edwards. Thank you for providing the friendliest, kindest, most generous kick-in-the-ass I have ever had the pleasure of receiving. I will never truly be able to repay you for what the two of you did for me, but please accept these few words as a symbol of my appreciation. I could not ask for two nicer (or better dressed) people to be in my corner.

To the rest of the Saugatuck crew: Leslie, Rima, Dora, Jody, Amanda, Jeff, Stephanie, Patti, Rose and Laura. I've said it before but it bears repeating: In a very real sense you too are partly responsible for the book you now hold in your hands. Thank you, my fellow misfits.

From the misty, distant past I'd like to thank Linda Murtagh although, back at Valley Stream South High School she was always *Mrs.* Murtagh. It was in her eighth grade public speaking class where I first found my voice, and later, in her drama club, where I put it to use. Teachers often wonder whether or not they make an actual difference in the lives of their students. Mrs. Murtagh: You made a difference. I thought you should know that.

To my parents, whose sole wish for me was to be happy: I am. *My* sole wish is that you could be here.

To Baxter, Maya and Molly, whose personalities, paw

prints and love are all over this thing, my life is so much better with you guys in it. So, stick around—things are just getting interesting.

Matty, thanks for making it so easy to be proud of you. CHOMP! CHOMP!

Emmy, thank you for being the gentle, sweet, funny person that you are. I never have, and never will write anything as beautiful as you. And, thanks for spotting that funny looking dog on the golf cart path back in Peachtree City. As deep as the ocean and as big as the sky. Always.

And, finally, to my amazing wife Melissa. Without your constant support *of* me, and faith *in* me—and I mean *constant*—this book simply would not be. It is truly a lucky man who can say that his best friend, biggest fan, wisest advisor and most ardent defender are all the same person. I *am* that lucky man. Thank you, babe. It's not mine; it's ours.

Contents

Contents

Some day, if I ever get a chance, I shall write a book, or warning, on the character and temperament of the Dachshund and why he can't be trained and shouldn't be. I would rather train a striped zebra to balance an Indian club than induce a Dachshund to heed my slightest command.

E. B. White

Preface: Dog Day of Summer

For as long as I can remember, whenever I heard the word *dog* I immediately thought of a solid, big-boned, heavily muscled, prodigiously drooling, wolflike mountain of mottled fur that wanted nothing more out of life than to be in my presence. This was partially due to a German Shepherd named King, who bore a remarkable resemblance to the creature I just described.

But mostly, it was due to my dad.

Back in the early nineteen seventies, my family and I spent a couple of summers at Highland Park, a bungalow colony that catered to Jewish families in upstate New York. For me it meant days filled with swimming, hiking, arts and crafts, softball, stickball, overnight campouts, and color war. In other words, it was a prepubescent boy's idea of nirvana. For my mom it meant sitting in an aluminum lawn chair, the kind with that ugly, woven fabric, in front of the bungalow with other mothers, talking about whatever mothers talked about in the nineteen seventies. I have a very vivid memory of the grown-ups concocting garbage cans full of sangria. That isn't an exaggeration; they actually used garbage cans! I probably should have been questioning the sanity, to say nothing of the legality, of creating thirty-five gallons of sangria at one time.

Instead I was trying to determine whether or not the garbage cans in which they concocted their bohemian brew were new cans, or simply hosed-out versions of the cans we used to store the remnants of our almost daily barbecues. At the time, I think I concluded that they were, indeed, new cans. Actually, I *prayed* that they were new cans. I also clearly recall that, for dads, summer at the bungalow colony still meant work.

During the week, everyone's father went to their regular jobs. Then, on Friday evenings, they endured the slow automotive exodus either toward the shores of Long Island or, as in my dad's case, toward the Catskill Mountains. Truth be told, the Catskills weren't very mountainlike. They were more like overachieving Jewish hills that if they applied themselves would one day—maybe—grow up to become big Christian mountains. So, our dad would arrive late Friday night, spend the next forty-eight hours immersed in chlorinated water, drowned in charcoal briquettes, numbed by thirty-five gallons of highly toxic, questionably prepared sangria, and then, late Sunday night, make the long drive back home to start all over again Monday morning.

I remember very clearly one steamy Friday evening during our second summer in Highland Park. It started with a phone call from my dad. I heard my mom's side of the conversation, but since this was long before the days of mobile or speakerphones, allow me a little literary license as I re-create my father's side of the conversation.

Dad: "I found a dog."
Mom: "Paul, you're not bringing a stray dog up here."

Dad: "I found him tied up in an abandoned store on my route. They left him to starve. You should see him— he's beautiful."

Mom: "Paul! Listen—you are *not* going to bring a stray dog up here. I mean it."

Dad: "Paula—"

Mom: "*Paul!!* I'm serious; do *not* bring a dog up here. Do you hear me?"

Dad: "*Paula*—"

[*Author's note*: Yes, my parents' names really were Paula and Paul. I know—it's cute. I now return you to my partially imagined phone conversation, already in progress.]

Mom: "Don't hang, *Paul*, don't you *dare* hang up...*Paul?*"

The bungalow we rented was basically one large bedroom, a bathroom, a small kitchen, and faded linoleum as far as the eye could see. My brothers and I slept on three single beds in the bedroom, and my parents slept on a trundle bed in what was essentially the dining area. Lying in our beds that night, doing a far from Oscar-worthy job of pretending to be asleep, we knew something big was going to happen when my dad got home. The telltale sound of tires slowly crunching on gravel told me that *some*thing had arrived.

Smack went the warped screen door, and then a little gasp escaped from my mom's throat. I think it's worth noting here that my mom wasn't much of a gasper. She was more a student of the yelling-bordering-on-screaming school of demonstrative exclamations—Brooklyn campus. But there *was* no yelling. In fact, there wasn't a sound. After a pregnant pause—and I mean, like, ten-days-past-due-date pregnant—and with no fanfare at all, the door to our bedroom slowly opened. Silhouetted from behind by the humming fluorescent light in the kitchen, entered a large, four-legged shadow. And I mean *large*, as in, *Are we absolutely sure this thing is a dog?*

My first instinct, which at the time, and even today, certainly seemed like the right call, was to crap in my pajamas. My second instinct was to lay deathly still and do everything in my power to prevent my first instinct from actually happening—which, I'll be honest with you, was very touch and go.

Play dead and he won't hurt you.

My weekly viewing of *Mutual of Omaha's Wild Kingdom* every Sunday night was finally paying big dividends. I knew that worked with black bears in Wyoming and Montana. I could only hope it would work in the Borscht Belt on whatever this thing was. I heard it slowly padding its way over toward my bed, its undoubtedly razor-sharp claws clicking menacingly against the tired linoleum. And then I felt the subtle sensation of a cool wetness brush against my right hand, which was hanging off the side of the bed.

Oh God! It's right next to me.

Stay still. Don't breathe.

And the no-crapping-in-your-pajamas thing still stands, Marlin Perkins.

And then it began to sniff me. It worked its moist, rubbery nose along each of my fingers, and then placed its muzzle in the cup of my palm, where, after a second or two, it loudly exhaled and broke contact with my skin. While my eyes remained welded shut, I didn't need to see the creature to know what it was now doing: Nothing. It was just standing there.

I could sense its largeness occupying the space in what was now a much smaller room. And just when I thought I would burst out in tears from the suspense, I felt a big, slippery tongue begin to slowly lick the back of my hand. Licks that at first felt coarse, but then caressing. In that moment, with the most common of canine gestures, this sad, stray creature which we would learn had been left to die alone, tied up in an abandoned bodega in Williamsburg, Brooklyn, ceased being a sad, stray creature and instead became our dog. And he was telling me, in the only way he knew how, that I had nothing to fear. That I could open my eyes and my heart. And if my family and I were game, he would gladly spend the rest of his life thanking us for saving it.

We were game. We named him King.

⚬ ⚬ ⚬

I never imagined that the feelings I had for King would still reside within me more than forty years later. To this day, every time my daughter Emily sees a German Shepherd, without fail she always asks, "Daddy, does he remind you of King?"

"Yes baby, he does," I always respond, never letting her know that every time she mentions his name my now grown-up heart still breaks a little. Although I think she sort of knows. She's a pretty smart kid. Which is why, for the life of me, I can't figure out how or why she got it into her head that she wanted a Dachshund.

Let's start with the obvious: Dachshunds just look odd.

It's like they were compiled out of spare dog parts that just happened to be lying around: the legs of a Chihuahua supporting the body of a Basset Hound that boasts the chest of a Boxer, with the bark of a Doberman. Let's be honest—this is a creature whose main claim to fame is its uncanny resemblance to a sausage casing containing subprime cow parts. Not exactly something to be proud of, in my book. But even that wouldn't bother me so much if it weren't for the Dachshund's attitude.

I'm pretty sure the phrase "He thinks his shit doesn't stink" was coined by a Dachshund owner. We all know that some men of short stature often possess what's known as a Napoleon complex. I think Dachshunds suffer from the same malady. There is a definite vibe that the vast majority of Doxies put out there, that says, in essence, *What are* you *looking at?* Which, oddly enough, just seems to make people want to look at them even more. People just seem to love their pluck; they admire their ability to seem bigger than their long and low bodies. They wonder how something so small, so oddly shaped, and so (some would say) undoglike in appearance somehow manages to consistently rank as one of the most popular dog breeds in the world. The answer, I believe, is that distinctly Dachshund attitude, an attitude that isn't directed solely at people. I've seen my Doxies around much larger dogs, ones that could easily seize them in their jaws and proceed to shake the attitude right out of them, but these beasts act as if *my* dogs were the canine equivalent of the Hells Angels. It's truly something to behold.

So how in the world did I, a former owner of a thoroughly Teutonic, gargantuan German Shepherd, come to own not one but *three* of these frankfurter doppelgangers?

You remember my daughter Emily, right?

As she sat giggling on the floor at the Dachshund breeder's house, her body blanketed in a writhing swarm of black-and-tan, six-week-old Dachshund puppies, I asked the question that every good daddy asks when confronted with a situation such as this: "Will you take a personal check?"

I never, ever considered myself a Dachshund person, and there are some days that I'm still on the fence. And I don't mean to imply that my Dachshunds represent *all* Dachshunds. They certainly do not. As with all dogs, they're as individual as the people who own them.

But over time, my Dachshunds have proven to me one, irrefutable fact: they are *not* hot dogs. And they don't take a backseat to any other breed of dog. They're simply, beautifully, and proudly just dogs. *My* dogs! My family. Solid, big-boned, heavily muscled, prodigiously drooling wolflike mountains of fur that want nothing more out of life than to be in my presence. Who am I to say no?

So thanks, Dad, for doing what was right.

Yes, Emmy, they always remind me of him.

And: good boy, King.

Very good boy.

HOUNDED

CHAPTER 1

Staring Contest, You and Me, GO!

I step across the threshold of the front door first; they follow, a submissive step behind me.

We begin our walk.

At 5:45, most of the neighborhood is still asleep. Until it awakens, the morning is ours. Today's forecast of sunshine is, at this early hour, a barely-there streak of pink above the treetops. My first intake of air feels like the first bite of a Granny Smith apple: crisp and sharp. As we move from driveway to sidewalk, a breeze winds through the trees, raining desiccated leaves of yellow and rust upon our heads. We start at a relaxed pace, allowing our bodies to adjust to being awake and in the weather. Each leash is loose, free of any tension, devoid of any restraint. They drape like fragile ribbons.

At six inches or so above the ground, their noses probe the air, taking in more discernible information in a sniff than I could in an interrogation. As we reach the bend in the road near the small field, a robin, obviously a recipient of the memo regarding the early bird catching the worm, pecks at the frosted soil for breakfast. We stop. They all turn their heads toward the robin. Their nostrils expand and contract. The robin freezes. For a moment, we're as still as a landscape. A second later, in a rush of feathers, the robin rises and flies over the bowed pines. In unison they exhale loudly, and we move on.

Farther along, one of our neighbors is walking out of his house with an insulated lunch bag hung on one shoulder and a hot cup of coffee in his hand, his car already idling at the curb.

"Morning. Out for an early walk?"

The four of us come to a slow stop. "Too nice of a morning to stay inside," I reply.

He kneels and begins to pet them. "Wow, they're really well behaved. No barking, no jumping. Hi, guys, how ya doin' today?"

"Yeah, well, we're having a good morning," I joke.

"You sure are," he says, as he continues to rub bellies and stroke ears. Then he says, "Well guys, I've gotta run. Have a good day, enjoy this weather."

"Will do. Come on, guys, let's go home."

He pulls away, and we are left once more under the boughs of shedding sycamores and in the silence of a hastening sunrise.

As we approach the skirt of our driveway we pick up speed and then glide to a soft stop by the garage doors. The leashes are as they began: limp and untangled. They each sit, tongues happily lolling sideways from the exertion, patiently waiting while I untether them from the nylon umbilical cords that connect me, in more ways than one, to them—and them to me.

"Stay," I instruct. The only parts of their bodies that move are their eyes. They're watching mine. I turn my back and walk up to the front door. I slide the key in, give it the necessary jiggle, turn the knob and swing the door wide. I look back at my three Dachshunds: Baxter, Maya, and Molly. They are stonelike and silent. I wait one more moment.

"Inside," I quietly say.

They rise from their haunches and walk—*not run*— but walk, as they should, through the front door. I pause a moment to look at the seasonal gift that is midautumn. I hear the clacking of nails on tile and the lapping of tongues on water. They are replenished. *I* am replenished. I say to myself, *That was a beautiful walk.*

"Hon."

"Beautiful walk."

"Babe."

"Walk."

"Matt, wake up!"

I pop up onto my elbow and the blanket and pillows tell me that I have gone nowhere. I'm in bed with my wife, Melissa— and once again, the dogs have entered my dreams.

"You okay?" she asks.

I take a swig of water from the bottle on my night table. "Yeah, I'm fine. Just dreamin'."

"Walk dream?"

I sigh. "I was talking again?"

3

"Yep. You gonna be able to fall back to sleep?"

"Yeah, sorry I woke you."

"It's okay, love you."

"Love you too."

I flip the pillow to the cool side and lay down again. I hear Melissa reconfigure herself in the sheets, facing away from me. We both settle in, once more, to the serious business of slumber.

Two minutes later I hear a single, sheet muffled word escape from my wife's once-again-drowsy lips: "Baxter."

I flip onto my side, punch the pillow, and whisper the same: "Baxter."

Baxter was our first Dachshund. We bought him from a breeder when we briefly lived just outside Atlanta. We got him when he was six weeks old, and he just turned five, so all totaled that's about four years and ten months of an exquisite kind of hell. Of course, to live with us for that amount of time Baxter must give all of us a great deal of joy, and he most certainly does. It's just that, well, that joy is usually tempered by moments of frustration, so pure and white hot, that it's amazing that he's lived with us for the past four years. And ten months.

Baxter is an extremely handsome dog. He has what's called in Dachshund circles a Roman nose: sizable, regal, straight as an arrow, two nostrils; it's—you know—a nose! He's a short-haired Dachshund, his coat soft and smooth to the touch; his ears feel closer to velvet than fur. He has a very deep, prominent chest, front paws the size of catcher's mitts, and incredibly muscular thighs, a fact made all the more remarkable when you take into account that Baxter has an activity level that fluctuates daily between that of a garden slug and a geranium. A *dead* geranium.

While originally bred in the 1800s in Germany to drag badgers out of their dens (*Dachshund*, in German, means "badger dog"), somewhere deep in Baxter's genetic makeup that particular gene—you know, the one that enables movement—has gone kaput, another German word that, loosely translated, means "Beggin' Strips eater." Yes, in a world where Dachshunds are categorized as either "mini," "tween," or "standard," Baxter is what one might call a "maxi." He's not a wiener dog as much as he is a bratwurst behemoth.

Every trip to the vet usually begins with my wife and I being admonished for feeding Baxter too much. We honestly don't. He's just, I don't know, big! I know the term is usually reserved for women of a certain physical type, but Baxter really is built like a brick shithouse. Run your hand along his body and you feel solid muscle. Granted, the muscle lies under a good inch of squishy, surprisingly comforting adipose tissue, but Baxter is still as solid as rock. Well, if that rock had a little give to it. The vet also reminds us that when lifting a Dachshund, it's very important to make sure that you support their backs, given their unique physical structure. I then remind the vet it's equally important, when lifting Baxter, that I support *my* back *due* to his unique physical structure. He is a load. But a deeply loved load. Although, he certainly doesn't make it easy—particularly on me.

Most mornings usually dawn with a twenty-five-pound black-and-tan blur landing smack on my chest where, after making sure all of my ribs are still intact, I endure a thorough face licking. And where most people are cognizant of their morning breath, Baxter fails to take that into consideration, bathing me in a noxious mixture of kibble, rawhide, and an underlying layer of something akin to dirt. Actually, now that my scent memory is kicking in, forget "akin to"—it *is* dirt! Baxter occasionally eats dirt. Not all of the time, but just enough so it's not unusual for me to emit a subtle, topsoil tang throughout the day. After my ritual cleansing, it's time for Baxter's morning constitutional, or as I've come to call it, the Walk of Shame. Mine, not his.

There is a reason I can only dream of walking all three of our dogs together: We did it in reality. *Once.* The reason why that one en masse walk turned so quickly from pleasant to problematic was indeed Baxter. Or, to be more specific, his highly inquisitive nose.

Every street sign and every mailbox, every blade of grass and every puddle, has a story to tell, and if there's one thing Baxter loves, it's a good story. The smellier the better. Maya and Molly are just as interested in the story; it's just that where Maya and Molly are content with skimming the blurbs on the book's back cover, Baxter's starting with chapter one and he's not moving until he gets to the acknowledgments in the back of the book. We walk three paces, and our canine convoy comes to a sudden, screeching stop as Baxter takes in the beguiling bouquet of a rock for the next sixty seconds. Three more paces, and he's investigating the aroma of a manhole cover. Maya and Molly are configured like they're right in the middle of a heated game of Twister, and Baxter is nostril deep in a search for some kind of olfactory forensic evidence. And then, to make matters worse, here comes my neighbor Gary with his three dogs. Look at 'em! Walking with the precision of newly minted marines, while Gary works those leashes like he's vying for the lead in the Iditarod. I'm nursing first- or possibly second-degree friction burns on my ankles, and Gary's walking and waving, smile on his face, like he's a balloon handler in the Macy's Thanksgiving Day Parade. With every precise paw step, his dogs are rubbing salt in my fresh, weeping wounds.

What should have been a pleasant, uneventful, fifteen-minute stroll around the block, turned into a forty-minute canine equivalent of a heated rugby match but with more pain and considerably less sportsmanship.

The terrible tangle of leashes, the relentless, auditory assault of multipitch barking, the insistent pulling toward every point of the compass: it was just terrible for Melissa and myself. The dogs survived, no worse for wear. Shortly after we managed to untangle the Gordian-like knot of collars and leashes—and debated whether or not the wounds on my ankles would leave a scar—Melissa and I were immersed in what can only be described as a sort of posttraumatic walk syndrome. The mere sight of those three, snakelike leashes hanging on the cold, metal hook in the garage was enough to set off a flashback to rival any from 'Nam, replete with the echoing jangle of actual dog tags, the accusatory, dagger-like eyes of my annoyed neighbors, and that relentless, awful barking!

The barking.

The barking.

And so, Baxter walks alone. It's for the best, really. Baxter gets the kind of one-on-one attention he requires, Maya and Molly avoid getting garroted by their own leashes, and every so often I get to dream of a walk that was like, well, simply a dream.

❦ ❦ ❦

When he's not following his nose into the wilds of suburban New Jersey, Baxter's days are filled with the kind of activities you'd expect him to have: nothing. Although, when the weather cooperates and the sun is out, you can often find him lying in the middle of the driveway working on his "black-and-tan."

When he's had his fill of sunbathing he retreats to the coolness of his club chair, where he spends the balance of his day sleeping, yawning, sleeping, stretching and other things that bear a striking resemblance to the act of sleeping. He'll occasionally sachet to the water bowl and, after a few lazy laps of his tongue make his way back to his chair where he'll continue his daily homage to the sin of sloth. And, that pretty much encapsulates Baxter's day. That is, until the sun goes down.

We call it his witching hour, although "bitching" hour would be just as appropriate. That's when we're reminded, in no uncertain terms, that Baxter is, like all dogs, a descendant of wolves. But there is no howling. No tearing at the grass or barking at the moon. No, Baxter's ancient ancestry manifests itself in a behavior that is as unique as it is unsettling: He stares.

At me.

Endlessly.

He doesn't do it to convince me to let him outside or to give him a treat or to get out of his chair—which, by the way, I used to consider *my* chair. I've arrived at the conclusion that Baxter stares at me for the sake of staring. And it gets to the point where it gives me the creeps. Do you have any idea how hard it is to watch a television program while being eyeballed by Buffalo Bill from *The Silence of the Lambs?*

It puts the tennis ball in my mouth or else it gets the hose.

He starts his assault from a distance of perhaps fifteen feet, his eyes boring into mine. And, the more I tell myself, "don't look at him," the more my eyes dart from the flatscreen to the black-and-tan rock. He advances slowly, almost imperceptibly. He takes one measured step. He stops. He stares. Motionless. It's like a scene from Animal Planet. Baxter, the dark and stealthy Dachshund, looks out upon the vast expanse of the Serengeti Plains (which, in this case, looks a lot like imitation wood floors), intent on his prey, me, a neurotic Jewish guy from Long Island, with a questionable flight response and a penchant for colorful language. Okay, it's not *exactly* like Animal Planet. Another quiet step. *Don't give him the satisfaction,* I try to convince myself. How many times was *I* told as a kid that staring is rude? After a few minutes of this abuse we've leapfrogged right over rude and landed on cruel and highly unusual punishment. He is, without a doubt, the most relentless, driven, focused dog I have ever met. He does not know the word *quit*. And when he does stop staring, it's simply because I've grown tiresome to him and not because he's feeling guilty about driving me almost to the point of neurosis. By the time Baxter is done with me, I'm a diminished, discarded, damaged toy.

It was during one of these typical staring/psychological torture sessions that I realized something. There was certainly nothing out of the ordinary about the moment: Baxter. Me. Staring. Just another round of ocular torment, typical stuff. But, for whatever reason, in a glance—one of thousands of glances at him—I saw something else, something that went beyond dog. When I looked in his eyes I saw *intent*. That all this time, he wasn't just staring at me simply because it amused him to mentally break a person—which, for the record, I *do* think he rather enjoys. This moment was something else: he was trying to tell me something.

His big, brown eyes locked on mine, Baxter had a message for me, something he felt I needed to know. Something that had nothing to do with getting *my* ass out of *his* chair. Now, excuse me while I wax anthropomorphically here, but I could swear that Baxter was speaking to me. Obviously not in words, but with a look. He was speaking in silence. He was most definitely trying to tell me something.

Turns out in this particular instance his staring was not torture: it was teaching.

And with an expression devoid of *any* expression, Baxter

was providing me with a lesson that I, for more years than I could count or care to remember, was in dire need of. Baxter was training *me*.

☙ ❧ ☙

Like most copywriters, I absolutely hate writing copy.

In my mind, writing marketing copy falls just below writing greeting cards but slightly above writing obituaries—and on some days, even that line is a rather hazy blur. And, as with most copywriters, I harbored a desire to write something beyond headlines and body copy. Even if what I had to say was of no interest to anyone else, I would feel fulfilled to write something that belonged solely to me. Well, maybe not fulfilled, but certainly better. *Probably* better.

But something often happens to writers, or, at least something happened to *this* writer: you start to seriously and regularly doubt your ability to write. It doesn't matter if other people acknowledge your ability; it doesn't matter if people refer to you as a writer. It doesn't even matter if your title is "writer." You sometimes stare at the words on the page and they seem false. They simply become a senseless, pointless series of upstrokes, downstrokes, and serifs.

They don't work. They don't even come close to capturing whatever it was you bled to express.

I suck!

Those are the words that best capture how I feel when to my eyes and my mind the lines on the page resemble nothing more than, well, lines on a page.

Write a book?

Uh, I don't think so.

Even as I write these words, words that may or may not be passing before someone's eyeballs other than my own, it seems laughable. I am sitting here looking at my fingers fly across the keyboard, and somewhere in the not-so-deep recesses of my mind I hear this:

Are you serious? You can't do this. Who are you to do this? You can't write a book: you write headlines. You don't have it in you, and even if by some miracle you do, there's no way you can get it out. You're stuck. You are and always will be a writer of advertising copy, not a writer of books. Stay in the shallow end of the literary pool, headline boy!

And that is where I have stayed: treading the piss-warmed, spit-infused, Band-Aid–clogged shallow end of the literary pool. Actually, right about now, composing obituaries doesn't sound all that bad.

And *that* is truly bad.

Shortly after I met my wife she gave me a copy of a quote attributed to Calvin Coolidge that she thought I would benefit from having, no doubt due to yet another session of my regularly scheduled crushing self-doubt:

Nothing in the world can take the place of persistence. Talent will not; nothing is more common than unsuccessful men with talent. Genius will not; unrewarded genius is almost a proverb. Education will not; the world is full of educated derelicts. Persistence and determination alone are omnipotent.

She gave me this quote about thirteen years ago. At the time, I thought it was total bullshit. Not the quote itself—it's a great quote with a great message. And I certainly didn't think my wife was bullshit for giving it to me. Like everything she did then, and everything she does today, she gave it to me out of caring and love for me. I say the quote was bullshit because I couldn't possibly see it applying to *me*.

That's a quote for people with real potential. People with an unwavering drive to be more than what people say they are; be more than what they believe they are. That wasn't me. It was a great quote being wasted on a not so great "writer": me.

And yet, I kept that quote.

Through three moves and lots of jobs, that piece of paper went along for the ride. As much as I failed to see myself in its poetry, I couldn't part with it. Maybe I thought that over time, and through some literary osmosis, that poetry would work itself into me. I don't know if my words have any more magic in them then they did thirteen years ago, but the tattered piece of paper is still with me.

It resides, at this very moment, about two feet over my left shoulder, where it holds a place of prominence on a bulletin board. It has watched me struggle. Watched me flagellate myself over my ability. Question my worth, my right to dream. And, on an average day, not unlike the day I am writing this sentence, that quote threw me for a loop.

🦴 🦴 🦴

I can't say exactly what day it happened. Epiphanies, as a rule, tend to occur when you least expect them. But I'm assuming it was an average day, because in life, well, most days nothing much epiphanylike happens. Except this one day, when the following five words suddenly, and inexplicably, found their way to the surface of my bottomless well of self-doubt:

Why can't I do it?

There is absolutely nobody holding me back except for that negative, moody guy staring out at me from the mirror every morning.

There were no fireworks, no burning bushes, no image of a literary messiah scorched in a burned piece of toast. Something finally, at long last, clicked. Sure, it may not have been an epiphany of biblical proportions, but it had teeth. I *could* write a book. I *would* write a book!

Phew! Glad we resolved that little problem.

Now, what the hell am I going to write about?

🦴 🦴 🦴

I'm staring at him, staring at me.

I'm sitting perfectly still.

He is sitting perfectly still.

I'm breathing.

I *think* he's breathing. It's hard to say.

"Baxter, tell Daddy what he should write about," I say to the silent sentinel.

He's got nothing.

That makes two of us.

I am stuck. Spinning wheels in the snow, slowly being swallowed by quicksand as dramatic music plays in the background, good and stuck. I have no idea what I am going to write about. Okay, I don't get this. For years I've known that I've had something inside me that needed to get out. Jonesing to get out! And, now that I've had this whole freaking epiphany thing, where I finally realized that I can indeed write a book, that I *do* have something to say, I sit here utterly clueless as to what exactly I should write! This whole epiphany thing has been nothing but a big tease.

"Baxter, *please*, stop staring at Daddy. You're giving me a complex," I implore. *"Baxter! STOP!"*

He steps a foot or so closer to me, his eyes locked on mine. He doesn't sit. He doesn't lie down. He just stands there, still as stone. It becomes one of those scenes in a movie, where the camera quickly cuts back and forth from one person to another, with the lens getting closer and closer with every transition, the music building, until...

"I swear, Baxter, you are the most annoying, persistent, determined dog I—"

(Yes, I stop yelling in midsentence, just like in the movies, dash and all.)

He takes one more tiny, hesitant step toward me.

He stares.

I stare.

That's it!

"Baxter, leave Daddy *alone*," my wife yells on my behalf.

"No babe, it's fine," I tell my wife, never breaking eye contact with Baxter.

It's *really* fine.

To paraphrase noted behaviorist B. F. Skinner:

If you want to know what a person is really thinking, don't listen to what they say, watch what they do.

In my personal experience, that also goes for dogs. At least the dog that stares at me like I'm a six-foot, steaming pile of beef brisket.

For the past four years (and ten months) he wasn't just staring: he was watching. Waiting. And he saw me doing absolutely nothing. Going absolutely nowhere. So, he did something about it. He showed me what persistence looked like. He was demonstrating what determination could get you. He was speaking to me and saying the same thing that my wife, in a gesture of love, told me thirteen years ago. That nothing, *absolutely nothing*, can take the place of persistence.

I had my book idea.

And my first Dachshund life lesson.

Dachshund Life Lesson #1

When the answer is staring you right in the face, stare right back.

CHAPTER 2

Be Quiet! And Speak.

From the very first day we adopted her from a breeder in Texas, Maya has done little to earn the reputation of a typical Dachshund. Whereas Baxter barks to be let outside, Maya will sooner soil herself than utter the slightest sound. Unlike Molly, who will whimper incessantly for a treat, Maya sits on the sofa, not unlike a throne, and patiently waits for the treat to be conveyed to her. And, while Baxter, as I said, wears the famed Dachshund attitude like a badge of honor, Maya seems to possess a complete and utter lack of that attitude. Which is not to say that Maya lacks personality, quite the contrary. It's just that where Baxter's personality is based on what he does, Maya's is based firmly on what she does *not* do.

Maya does not come when you call her; Maya will join you when, and if, she feels like joining you.

Maya does not lay down: Maya's body will ease itself into a prone position when she determines that there is nothing much worth standing for, which seems to be most things.

Maya can hear perfectly: she just doesn't care to listen.

She has the ability to bark, yet she reserves her bark for situations she deems bark-*worthy*, such as: the sound of a door opening, the sound of a door closing, the garage door opening, the garage door closing, somebody coming down the stairs, someone going up the stairs, a car pulling into the driveway, the same car pulling out of the driveway, the doorbell ringing, a lawn mower starting, a dog barking two miles away and a mouse farting in the woods under a log during a thunderstorm. But, she never, ever barks to bring any type of attention or, for that matter, kindness to herself. It's as if she's barking purely to fulfill her contractual obligation as a dog, and not a "Ruff," "Yelp," or "Arf" more.

The truth of the matter is that, for most of the twenty-four hours in a day, Maya is quietly observing the world going on around her. And, I'm sad to say, I think that stems from her past.

🦴 🦴 🦴

We don't know much about Maya's life before she became a part of ours. When we started to think about adding another mouth to the Ziselman litter, we began researching various Dachshund breeders across the country. We also thought that it might be nice to adopt an older Doxie. Melissa found a breeder in Texas with an attractive, respectable-looking website. We started looking at the different dogs available in the "For Sale" section of the site. Most were adorable puppies; there were also some dogs for sale that were a year or so old. But, there was one dog, considerably older than the rest that was also for sale. It said she was six years old. Her muzzle was already heavily tinged with white, and, to my eyes, she seemed a bit on the scrawny side. Her black-and-tan fur was neither long nor short, but somewhere in the middle. But what I remember the most was her expression. She looked somber, as if she was somehow unworthy of having her picture taken. And, at $200, she was the least expensive dog on the site. Ironically enough, we would soon consider her priceless. Her name was Maya.

We sent an e-mail to the breeder, telling them of our interest in Maya. The breeder sent a rather lengthy response, inquiring as to what we were looking for in a Dachshund, and, in particular, who would be the main caregiver to the dog. We replied that we wanted a dog that was mature, quiet, calm, and nonaggressive, and that we would all be taking care of the dog. The breeder responded and said that Maya would be a perfect fit. We said that it sounded great, but that we wanted a few days to think about it. She said that would be fine.

We didn't end up needing a few days. We had already fallen in love with Maya and were eager to bring her to her new home. We sent the breeder an e-mail with the news and asked her to respond as soon as possible to expedite the process. A day or two passed with no response. Then another day. And one more. Then, about five days after we sent the e-mail, our phone rang: it was the breeder (we had supplied our phone number in a previous e-mail). She apologized profusely for not responding faster. She said that she had been very ill, which was why she was giving up all of her dogs. Even over the phone, her love for her Doxies was palpable. Melissa and I felt terrible for this woman. She assured us that Maya was the sweetest dog in the world, and we assured her that we would treat the sweetest dog in the world in the manner that she so richly deserved. No sooner had we made payment and travel arrangements, and hung up the phone, when Melissa burst into tears.

"Oh my god, I feel absolutely awful for that woman."

"I know. Obviously, she's one of those people who just loves animals and would do anything for them. It's good we're doing this. We'll give Maya a great life."

"Maybe it's meant to be that we take care of Maya," Melissa suggested.

"I think you're right. Now, comes the hard part. C'mon, let's break the news to Baxter that he's no longer an only Dachshund."

There is a word in Yiddish, *bashert*, which means "fate" or "destiny"; Maya was *bashert*.

And she was on her way.

❦ ❦ ❦

Waiting at the airport to pick up Maya I imagined us sitting side by side on the sofa during cold, winter nights, stroking her soft ears while her mere presence calmed and soothed my constantly addled mind. After a long wait a baggage handler brought Maya out to the waiting area. While we *oooh*ed and *aaah*ed at the now-familiar face staring at us through the wire door of the carrying crate, it was immediately apparent that Maya was not only scared but, of even greater concern, scarred. Not physically but emotionally.

She cowered toward the back of the carrier. She displayed no pent-up excitement at the thought of being released after a three-hour flight from Houston. Where other dogs in carriers were barking furiously, straining the locks on their carriers to their limits, Maya seemed content to keep the bars of her carrier firmly between us and her. As slowly, and as quietly as possible, I unlatched the lock on the carrier and gently slid my hands around her back and midsection. As I extracted her from the carrier I was thinking to myself, *She feels too thin.* She exited the carrier with her toes splayed, her tail tucked firmly between her legs, and her back hunched. I placed her on the floor in front of us. To my eyes her back seemed somewhat twisted, not quite right. She looked fragile. While Emily stroked Maya's face and back with excitement, Melissa and I shared a quick, concerned look at each other. "Okay, let's put her leash on and get her out of here," I said with a note of urgency in my voice.

"Daddy, is everything okay?" Emmy asked me, picking up on my worried tone.

"Yeah baby, I just want to get her out of all of this noise. C'mon, let's take her to her new home." As I merged onto the turnpike I knew that noise would be the least of Maya's issues. Releasing her from her cage would be the easy part; releasing her from her past would be the real challenge.

My wife and I brought her upstairs that first night to lie down between us in bed, in an attempt to offer her some subdued comfort after, what must have been for her, a long, stress-filled flight to a new life. She quickly settled in between us while we slowly stroked and rubbed her white-tinged muzzle. She didn't make a sound. She wouldn't look at me.

She didn't budge.

Not a ripple of life passed under our fingers. Except for the warmth softly radiating from her body, we could have been stroking the cold marble of a statue. While I didn't, and would never know, the kind of life Maya lived before she came to us, I knew that for a dog to behave like this, it must have been less than stellar and, quite possibly, closer to miserable. I felt terrible. I also felt lied to. Did the breeder mislead us on purpose? Was she simply eager to unload an old dog with serious behavioral issues? Was the breeder even really sick? While I didn't share my thoughts with Melissa, I knew she was battling the same doubts. I felt terrible thinking like that. I want to think the best of people, especially those who portray themselves as "dog people." On the phone, the breeder sounded genuine in her concern in finding just the right home for Maya. I mean, she really sounded like she loved her! But, that first night, it was hard to see any remnant of love, or spark of light, in Maya's eyes.

This wasn't just an older dog: it was a dog aged by circumstance. She wasn't gentle: she was frozen by fear. Of course she was nonaggressive; aggression was a behavior and this dog didn't exhibit any kind of behavior: she just...existed. Barely. In the beginning when she wouldn't come near me it just about broke my heart.

Jesus, Maya, what did they do to you? ran through my mind those first few, difficult days. What kind of life, what kind of treatment, would eradicate a dog's innate desire for human companionship? We quickly realized that she didn't fear just *people*—she feared *everything*. I wanted to cry. I *still* want to cry. She is marked with the worst kind of scars; the kind you can't see. And there is no balm to soothe the pain, to diminish the bruises of time.

Whenever any of us picks up Maya, she tends to moan and groan. I'm sure part of it comes from age; lord knows I can attest to that. As I write this Maya is three months past her ninth birthday. But I think part of the reason for her moaning, a not-inconsequential part, is her past. They are moans of memory.

After a while Maya warmed up to all of us, but it was a thaw at a glacial pace. Eventually, in a total act of submission, she rolled on her back, allowing us to gently rub her soft belly. Generally speaking there's not much to look at on a dog's belly, but with Maya being a girl, her nipples were pronounced. If there is such a thing as a sad nipple, well, then Maya's nipples are sad. They're flat. They're shriveled relics. They look like they have been overburdened with the birth of countless litters. They look like they've been through a war. And lost.

How much attention was she expected to provide to all of her puppies, while receiving who knows how little attention and nurturing herself? Her nipples, like her eyes, were just lifeless.

Her silence is also a relic. A sad souvenir of an empty existence, absent of everything, and anything, that makes a dog's life full. Her silence, and her choice of never bringing attention to herself—I think—stems from where she was born and how she was raised. And what she was used for.

She is a pained dog. A wronged dog. And yet, under the pain, I have always sensed something else. I've felt it from day one with Maya. Call it a kind of wisdom. A wisdom that comes from seeing and experiencing things that, while horrific, imbue a certain kind of awareness that others who haven't gone through that experience lack. I don't know what Maya endured, only that she did just that: endured. Like all good soldiers, Maya earned her stripes.

🦴 🦴 🦴

There is a saying that goes:

"The smart man speaks; the wise man listens."

Maya is not the smartest of our dogs; I think Baxter, for all of his mischief and attitude, takes that title. But I have no doubt at all that Maya is the wisest. And whether she realizes it or not, she has reinforced for me something that I always believed, something that unbeknownst to me, I actually *subscribed* to. That silence is not just golden: it's a life strategy.

🦴 🦴 🦴

People have always said that I don't talk enough. Teachers, girlfriends, coworkers, my mom, all of them told me I needed to say more. Funny, I always thought that I talked exactly as much as I needed to. It's like saying you don't breathe enough.

When I was about fourteen, my mother suggested I take a public speaking course to "bring me out of my shell." So, being the introverted mollusk that I was, I took the class. And it did something to me. I heard my voice. Actually, I was surprised to learn that I *had* one! And yet, for the most part, I still remained silent.

Through jobs and relationships, sadness and joy, I opted to

25

listen. Make no mistake, when I had something to say I said it. And still they would ask, "Why don't you talk more?" My response? Dead air.

In the early days with my soon-to-be wife, my brother Steven shared a sentiment with her that stayed with her to this very day. He said something to the effect of:

"My brother might not talk much, but when he does, you should listen."

While I certainly appreciated my brother's kind words, I disagreed with what he said. Who the hell am I? I have no great lessons to impart. I'm just a guy who doesn't talk a lot. Who's to say that I'm not just being linguistically lazy? Maybe I just don't see the point in making much ado about nothing. *Any* ado! Or, maybe I have my own bruising memories, my own scars that mute my voice. I know a girl from Texas with the same condition.

❦

You can't help but look at Maya and sense that she knows something the other dogs don't. Sure, generally speaking, you grow wiser as you grow older, or at least you hope you do, and Maya is a mature dog. But there's something more going on with Maya. As if her experiences have earned her a pass. Where she isn't required to "speak" or do things other dogs do. She's barked all of her barks. She has filled her quota of "heel," "fetch," and "shake hands," if not in practice then certainly in spirit. In short, Maya has earned her silence. And my respect.

While my wife always says that Baxter is "my" dog, it's

really in Maya's eyes that I see myself reflected. She keeps to herself. She is comfortable in her own company. She prefers things quiet. She seems completely content doing much of nothing. Breathing. Gazing. Just being. That's Maya. That's also me. Who knows? Maybe I too have earned the right for others to consider me wise. Well, maybe, on a really good day, when I've got my A game going, wise-*ish*?

Perhaps we've all earned the right to consider ourselves wise. Pain is not a proprietary thing. It's certainly not species specific. It's everywhere, in everyone. But do we learn from that pain? Do we burnish those lessons to a fine luster over the passage of time, to yield some great wisdom upon which we can rest our weary minds and broken hearts? Maybe. I don't know. I'm just a copywriter who doesn't talk much. I suppose that's an answer only we as individuals can answer. As for myself, I'm fortunate to have a teacher.

One who reminds me every day that some kinds of wisdom, maybe even the most important kind, are not spoken, and yet they are clearly heard. They are not at first blush seemingly profound, and yet they're as meaningful as anything else our parents imparted to us when we were young.

I will never know what Maya left behind and, quite honestly, I'd rather not dwell on it. It makes reading even these words far too painful. But I feel her past when I touch her fur. I hear it in her moans. About the only thing I can do at this point in her life, as well as in mine, is my very best to keep her healthy and happy. I will do all that I can to ensure that she never know the burden of worry, fear, pain, or want the rest of her days.

I don't think she's listening, but just in case she is, this is my message to my Maya:

Let *me* worry for you. Let *me* carry your burden. Let your back feel nothing but the sun and the promise of more days too numerous to count. And I will gain wisdom from the love of a mature, quiet, gentle girl.

I hear every word you never say, Maya. I hear nothing.
I hear it all.

Dachshund Life Lesson #2

Listen, especially when there's nothing to hear.

CHAPTER 3

The Clock Is Licking

It's often been said that one of the things that separates humans from animals is that humans know they are going to die. Dogs don't have the mental capacity to understand the concept of self, which makes it impossible for them to understand that their self has an expiration date to be determined at some point in the future. I'm not so sure I agree.

Certainly there's considerable research and evidence that elephants not only understand the concept of "dead," but that they actually grieve when one of the herd succumbs. I'm in no position to defend or negate either premise. I'm just a guy with three Dachshunds. But I'll tell you this: I think Molly knows that one day she is going to die. Here's why I think this:

She's unapologetically, consistently, reliably happy.

I don't know if her adorably diminutive size contributes to her constant air of perkiness, but, Molly is, far and away, the most happy-go-lucky, glass-is-half-full, the-sun-will-come-out-tomorrow dog I've ever been around. If there's such a thing as a canine, cockeyed optimist, she lives under my roof. I can be having the crappiest kind of day, but one look at Molly and the crap—at least for a little while—is forgotten. She cavorts like a fool, eats like a pig, and sleeps like a baby. She scampers, barks, and writhes in freshly mown grass as if it's the most amazing thing to do on one's back. When it comes to being a dog, Molly is all in. Which is why I think she knows.

She lives as if she knows for a fact that her time with us is finite. That she will not be here to see my daughter get married or watch as my body continues its slow decline toward my golden years. She seems as if she's trying to squeeze as much joyful happiness into the years she has left.

I look at Molly and I can't help but smile. She's just one of those dogs. But it's a smile that is always tempered with the sadness of the inevitable. Or, maybe I'm sad because I have such trouble living like she lives. Living with complete abandon and relishing everything I see, hear, smell, and experience.

Would I be that way, *could* I be that way, if I knew that my lifetime would, in all likelihood, not span more than a baker's dozen of years...if that? That's too hard to say and far too depressing to ponder. But, I look at my Molly, blissfully squirming in a pile of god-knows-what in the backyard, and I can't help but think she's trying to let me in on a little secret.

What else is new?

🦴 🦴 🦴

Crankenstein.

That's what my wife and daughter call me from time to time. Okay, they call me it a lot! The fact that I am prone to being cranky is probably the world's worst-kept secret. I freely admit to being an occasional moody pain in the ass. Granted, "pain in the ass" doesn't have the poetic lilt or the literary inspiration of "Crankenstein," but so be it. Pain in the ass is what I am.

I don't go out of my way to be moody. It's not something I put on my to-do list. Lots of times I'm not even aware I'm *being* moody. But there seems to be no shortage of people who are all too willing to alert me to my moodiness. Hey, I agree with them! You're preaching to the choir! Look, I'm not proud of being moody, but I'm certainly not ashamed of it. It's simply the cut of my cloth. Cranky cloth.

Some of the words, although certainly not a complete list, that often pop up when describing yours truly are:

Negative
Pessimistic
Uncaring
Angry
Somber
Crotchety
Disengaged
Caustic
Unapproachable
Miserable

I would probably add *complaining* and *fatalistic*.

Wow, I really *am* a bit of a prick, aren't I?

"Why can't you just be more positive, and try not to always see the negative?" my wife implores me on an almost-daily basis.

I'm not really sure, babe, but, since we're batting around

the idea of changing the very essence of who we are, why can't you be taller? Change your blood type? Or, I don't know, grow an eleventh finger?

Point, Matt!

🦴 🦴 🦴

This is me.

You take the good with the bad. I can only hope that the good outweighs the bad, and since we've been married almost twelve years, I feel pretty confident that it has. That, or my wife is just a glutton for punishment.

I don't know why I am the way that I am. Who the hell *does*? Look, I'm not the most devout person on the planet, but in terms of wreaking havoc on the Ten Commandments my record's pretty respectable. And, as far as I know, "Thou shalt not be such a negative son of a bitch" didn't make the final cut.

So, I'm not big on smiling—big deal! Every night the evening news brings us a fresh list of horrors happening around the world, and there are people in that same world who are actually stressed out over the fact that I'm not cracking a *smile*? Seriously? People, get your priorities in order: war, famine, climate change, political upheaval, crumbling infrastructure, overpopulation, economic crises, and overreliance on foreign oil. *Then* comes the fact that I don't smile a lot! To me, that's a much more sensible list of priorities.

"You know, it takes more muscles to frown than it does to smile," I've often been reminded of.

Fascinating.

Hey, you know what utilizes even fewer muscles than smiling? Raising a middle finger into a vertical position—that's practically effortless. It's true! I can vouch for it.

To those tortured souls who worry about me, who wish that I were different and not so quick to go over to the dark side. I'm with you. Honestly, I wish I wasn't so moody, too, and didn't give off the whole "unapproachable" vibe. It's exhausting. Physically and mentally. But I do. Hey, it could be worse. I have to deal with me 24/7: you're just a temporary visitor to MattLand. My advice? Keep your hands inside the car at all times, no flash photography, and please, try not to do anything that's going to, you know, upset me. No, I *can't* tell you what that might be, but, hey, that's part of the fun, right? Enjoy your ride!

🦴 🦴 🦴

But, as of late, even *I've* been getting to me.

So I think it's time to at least try to temper the moodiness and reduce the negativity. Do whatever I can to change my ways and if not eliminate my negativity altogether, then at least mute it a bit. It's time to bring in the big guns, which just happen to belong to our littlest dog.

I'm going to channel Molly.

I'm going to use Molly as my mood guide, my sensei in my transformational journey to be less like me. I'll simply do as she does and, hopefully, come out the other end feeling happier, more at peace, more Molly-*ish*.

I'll need total quiet, please.

Let us begin:

• Effective immediately, whenever possible, I'm going to run around in circles as if chasing imaginary butterflies. This will allow me to get in touch with my inner child and, if I'm lucky, provide me with a cheap buzz that occurs as a result of running around in circles as if chasing imaginary butterflies.

• Weather permitting, I will bask in the sun with a complete and utter disregard for skin cancer and the appropriate level of SPF protection. This will allow me to absorb the positive vitamins that one typically derives from sunlight and avoid, at least temporarily, the lectures one usually gets from one's overly alarmist dermatologist.

• Starting today, I will bark every time I hear a doorbell, a cell phone, a car horn, a clap of thunder, a strange voice, a car engine starting, or a microwave oven timer going off. And I don't just mean bark once. I am going to bark incessantly. Like, in five-minute chunks. Not only will this be good practice in terms of heightening my senses, it will give the illusion to all who hear me that we actually have a full-sized dog in the house, and not just, well, you know.

• When encouraged, I will roll on my back, with my legs akimbo, and let people rub my torso, starting between my nipples and going all the way down to my bellybutton. That's pretty much self-explanatory.

• During the colder months I will sleep naked next to a heating duct. This will keep me warm and comfortable and, for once, eliminate the need to wrestle my wife for the comforter.

• Every night, before I go to bed next to my heating duct, I will spend approximately three to seven minutes arranging my old, tattered throw blanket. This not only creates a softer spot on which to sleep, but also allows me to showcase my exceptional folding skills gained during my short-lived stint in retail.

• And, finally, rather than relieve myself in the toilet, as society would have me do, I will begin urinating in the corner of the dining room. Doing so will not only enable me to connect with my dormant, childlike innocence and purity of heart, it will…actually, the "innocence and purity of heart" thing is pretty much the only upside to this one. The rest is just nasty.

Aaaah, I feel happier already.

🦴 🦴 🦴

As with any person who loves their dog, I don't want to think about the day that is out there in the misty distance: the day when Molly will have used up her allotted time in our lives. Far too sad. And, as much as I wish I had the power to keep that day at bay, I obviously don't.

But I try not to dwell on it. Instead I revel in watching a seemingly oblivious yet perfectly happy Dachshund go about living her life as if each day was the best day ever.

I think she might be on to something.

Dachshund Life Lesson #3

If you're going to be moody, "Happy" is a pretty good choice.

CHAPTER 4

After You, Bitch!

It is a tale told completely in body language.

He aims his nose toward the ground as he slowly stalks his prey. His eyes constantly scan the immediate area, searching for anything that can be perceived as a threat, yet his head remains steady, his gaze never wavering far from the object of his attention.

At just a few inches away from his unsuspecting victim, his pace slows, his head gradually begins to rise and, in a leap reminiscent of his long-ago ancestors, he lands with surprising force just above his quarry's shoulder...

...and proceeds to hump the crap out of it.

Baxter: cautious, cunning—and apparently lacking even a rudimentary grasp of Dachshund physiology.

I've read about it and asked about it, and I've watched *The Dog Whisperer*: it's about dominance. In the dog world, nothing says *I'm in charge* like trying to impregnate another dog's scapula. Of course there's the urine marking, the growling, and the staring, all of which are the dog equivalent of *Don't even think about it*.

But in our home, Baxter carries about as much weight as

an anorexic flea. For all of his bruising posturing and blustery barking, Baxter is low dog on a very short totem pole. And I think he knows it, which is what makes watching his faux dominance so thoroughly entertaining to watch.

Hey Dad, watch me go right up to Maya's food bowl and grab the last bits of her kibble, he says to me in a determined glance, a determination that will quickly whither before my eyes as Maya, with a startling display of incisors, foils Baxter's deeply flawed plan.

Hey Dad, check this out. I'm going to walk right up to Molly and take that rawhide stick right out of her mouth, okay—watch this. Dad! Are you watching? Okay, watch.

What I *actually* watch is Baxter's wide load being forcefully driven down the stairs by a twelve-pound Dachshund with the bravado and balls of a Bull Mastiff.

And, of course, you're not doing your rep any favors when you can't control your bladder. Yes, when Baxter gets really excited he…well, let me put it this way: you can look only so tough while dribbling a Jackson Pollock across the kitchen floor.

But as I'm trying my best not to laugh right in his muzzle, I can't help but think that dominance, when viewed from a different angle, looks an awful lot like manners.

For instance, when Baxter has to wait his turn at the water bowl because Molly arrived there the same time that he did, it sort of looks like he's allowing her to drink first. Such a gentleman, although the truth is that when it comes to eating and drinking, Baxter gives Molly a very wide berth. But you know, it does sort of look like he's being polite to the lady.

After everyone has done their business outside, Baxter

and Molly rush to the door where Molly, without fail, enters first. And while it's actually me who's holding the door open, it appears as if Baxter is *allowing* Lady Molly to cross the threshold before he does. Who says chivalry is dead? In reality, it's Baxter who would be dead if he dared to usurp Molly's place at the front door.

You may be wondering where Maya is while all of this scary glaring and physical posturing is going down. She is, in all likelihood, laying on her back in the driveway in complete and utter submission to me. I will then pick her up and carry her into the house, where she then takes her place on either the big blue floor pillow or the pillow on the sofa, also known as her throne. Don't ask: it's a whole other chapter. (That's not just a figure of speech; it really is a whole other chapter, so keep reading.)

He's a dog. I *know* he's not deferring to Molly and Maya—I get it. I'm just saying that, I don't know, maybe I wish it *were* manners that I was witnessing. I mean, what's the harm in thinking that? It's not like there's a surplus of manners in the world right now, even though we could sure use one.

Maybe Baxter is telling me, in his inimitable way, that even in the dog-eat-dog world of *being* a dog, maybe manners *should* matter. They certainly matter in mine.

Ah, here comes the next paragraph. Please, after you! No, no, I insist.

❧ ❧ ❧

If you want to piss off my wife—although I don't know why you'd want to go and do something like that; she's a lovely woman, and after all, you barely know her—don't hold the door open for her. If you are leaving a department store just ahead of my wife, and you, for whatever reason, don't hold that door open for her and you let it slam in her face, well, don't say I didn't warn you.

"What the hell is wrong with people? Did she not see me two steps behind her? It's common courtesy. I swear, every day I'm out in the world my faith in my fellow man goes down another peg!"

As I said, I'd hold the door.

And I would most definitely thank her if *she* holds the door open for *you*.

"Oh, you're welcome, my pleasure," she grumbles under her breath as the person who just passed through the door that she was holding open walks away, blissfully unaware that he or she has awakened a sleeping volcano, and that the volcano will feel compelled to discuss this incident, ad nauseum, right when the volcano's husband is trying to go to sleep. But not to worry, it will all even out in the end. You see, ours is a two-volcano home.

I don't recall being raised in an overly polite home. I suppose, like most kids, we were taught the meat-and-potatoes of manners: "Always remember to say *please*, *thank you*, and *you're welcome*." I also don't remember taking it too much to heart, but for some reason, it stuck with me.

In my adult life I always do my very best to be polite. It costs me nothing, it makes me feel good about myself, and there's always the chance that the person I'm extending polite-ness *to* will, in turn, spread that politeness around.

A small, ever-shrinking chance.

Manners just don't seem to be what they were once upon a time: abundant.

There once was a time when manners and proper etiquette were actually taught in classes. They were assumed. Today, it's a rare day indeed when more than a single person extends a courtesy my way. Whenever my wife and I go out to dinner and, by some alignment of the planets, we receive exemplary service, we always go out of our way to let the manager know, for the simple and sad reason that it happens so infrequently. A job well done is, in my eyes, another kind of politeness: a politeness that comes from doing exactly what's expected of you. And if there is one area of life where manners have all but flown bye-bye it is, appropriately enough, in the area of air travel.

When I buy an airline ticket I know that the plane will not leave for its destination without me. Barring some unforeseen error on my part, like oversleeping or not leaving enough time to get to the airport, that plane will remain at the gate until I make my way to my assigned seat. And that's not just a cour-tesy extended to me by the airlines because I'm something special, because I'm certainly not—a fact that the airline will go out of its way to remind me of once we're airborne.

So I never quite understand why people feel compelled to adopt a herd mentality in order to barge, shove, push, and rush their way onto a plane that isn't going to move an inch until we're all aboard anyway.

I am no student of aeronautical engineering—indeed, I'm still always amazed that something so big and heavy can get and remain airborne. However, I *do* know that every seat on a plane arrives at the intended destination *at the same time*!

Those ropes that festoon the boarding area like Christmas garland are not meant to act as a starting line in your race to forced confinement. They are meant to remind and encourage people to partake in the boarding process in an orderly and systematic fashion. While they may not be velvet, those ropes are soft reminders to behave, to be considerate of your fellow passengers. Take your time and listen to the instructions from the gate attendant, and we'll make this process a lot more tolerable.

And to the pituitary case sitting in front of me:

The plane doesn't end where you're sitting, my friend. There's a whole world of crying babies and questionable hygiene sitting behind you, to say nothing of your fellow brethren who also never met an all-you-can-eat buffet they didn't like.

But, most important, *I* am behind you, and I would appreciate it beyond measure if you would remember that fact, particularly when you're attempting to recline your seat past the point where it has been carefully calibrated in a factory *not* to go beyond. You see, while I don't plan on having any more children, I've grown attached to my testicles and they to me. If nothing else, they help dress the front of my pants. So, your pushing the back of your seat in an attempt to give yourself more room will achieve nothing but making my ginger ale slosh over the rim of the cup, leaving me with a sodden cocktail napkin and minipretzels that bear little of their original crunch.

I could just as easily lean back as the dude in front of me, but I don't. Know why? Because, as uncomfortable as I might be, and I always am, I am not about to inflict such rudeness on the person behind me.

If I do feel the need to recline I always peek around the side and inform the person behind me that I'm going to recline and that, if I recline back too far, to let me know and I will move it forward a bit. I know—I am a remarkably awesome human. In truth, I'm not; I'm just trying to be considerate to someone who is as uncomfortable as I am. Sadly though, I'm a minority of one at thirty-five thousand feet.

On a recent trip into Manhattan I was planning on taking a cab to my office near Union Square. In front of Penn Station there is a taxi stand where, if you wait on line long enough, you will eventually get a cab. I waited in line. My turn to enter a cab was at hand. And then a woman proceeded to jump in my cab, suitcase in tow, and the cab left.

I did not yell at the woman. I did not curse out the cab-driver because all he's interested in is a fare, and my knowledge of Farsi is rudimentary at best.

Know what I did?

I laughed.

Not because it was funny but because it was the quintessential act of rudeness and ill manners. You see it happen in movies all the time, but I've never experienced it myself. Trust me, I was pissed, but at some level I actually felt sorry for the woman who stole my cab. She was on her way to wherever she was on her way to, clueless to the fact that she just treated someone so badly. Odds are good she's the kind of person who doesn't care how she treats people anyway. It's all about her. The world's full of them. I caught the next cab without incident and I made my meeting, but the cab heisting stayed with me the rest of the day.

That evening, after I had a chance to decompress from the nightmare that is commuting into Manhattan from central New Jersey, I was sitting outside just watching the dogs.

It was the kind of summer evening you wish you could make several copies of and pull one out whenever you were so inclined. There was no barking, no cars driving by, and the only intrusion, if you could even consider it that, was the periodic glow emanating from a firefly's ass. It was a moment of calm in a day that was in short supply of it.

"Let's go guys, *inside*," I said to the dogs.

All three raced to the door knowing full well that *inside* meant "night-night" cookies, sans milk, and a bunch of goodnight kisses. As I was about to open the screen door to let them in, I noticed that Baxter, who arrived first at the door, slowly shifted into reverse, thereby allowing Molly and Maya to enter first. And in the time it took me to say to Melissa "Did you see that?" the girls raced inside with Baxter bringing up the rear. Again.

He might not be the toughest Dachshund in the neighborhood; truthfully, he's not even the toughest Dachshund in the *house*. And yes, he caves at the slightest threat from the girls. But Baxter has his moments of kindness.

All right, all right, I *know* that it's not really kindness he's exhibiting; he's simply being submissive. It's *me* that's seeing kindness and gentility and doing the right thing, because I want to see it. And on very trying days, like the day with the cab and the no good, horrible, very bad lady who stole it, I *need* to see it.

When *Thank you* is in short supply and *No, please, after you* isn't showing up anytime soon, I desperately need to believe that even a Dachshund with a potential inferiority complex and a weak bladder knows that manners matter.

Dachshund Life Lesson #4

Be polite. You'll always make someone's day.

CHAPTER 5

Poop du Jour

I could probably assemble a sizable group of people who would, when asked, testify to the fact that over the course of my professional life I have written a lot of crap. In fact, I'd probably put myself at the head of the line in that little focus group. But, nobody could ever accuse me of writing *about* crap, at least not intentionally. (Wait for it...)

Until now.

Its technical name is *coprophagia*. And, like some old Amish tenet, we dare not speak of it in public. We're more or less safe at PetSmart. But I'm going to speak of it:

Maya sometimes eats poop.

And when she's caught doing it, I could swear that she looks like she's smiling. Yes, when Maya chows down on some newly minted turds she literally displays a shit-eating grin. I've been in advertising for more than twenty years. I've figuratively taken more crap than I can count. But I can't recall ever cracking a grin over it, not even a little.

There are several theories floating around as to why some dogs feel the need, bordering on obsession, to eat another dog's, and sometimes their very own, feces.

The first applies just to female dogs, or (in the parlance of official doggie-dom), bitches. Go ahead, start your giggling, you're in good company. I'm as guilty as the next guy of laughing at the commentator at a dog show, when he says, "This cocker spaniel is a young, but really impressive-looking bitch."

"Daddy, is he allowed to say that?" my daughter Emily asks.

"Yep, that's what they call girl dogs."

"Well…what do they call *boy* dogs?"

"They just call them boy dogs, baby."

Couple seconds' pause.

"But that's not really nice."

I'm not sure who came up with the idea of calling female dogs bitches or the reasoning behind it, but it kind of makes me believe that whoever that person was, they really weren't putting their all into it. On my worst, least creative, laziest day, with my eyes closed, I think I could have done better than *bitch*:

Girlie dog?

Cutie-pie?

Not great, but certainly much more palatable and less off-putting than *bitch*. Although, let's face it, it does afford us one of those very rare times in life when you can use a bad word in a certain context and have it be totally innocent.

Like when you get a new cock for your henhouse, or when you're sewing and you give yourself a little prick. And, of course, who can deny the pleasure derived from watching a bunch of asses frolic in a grassy meadow?

But let's get back to the bitches and why some of them eat crap, shall we?

The first theory has to do with a dog's wolf heritage.

Wolves, while certainly badasses in their own right, weren't necessarily the biggest badasses. That distinction went, and continues to go, to bears. Consequently, whenever a wolf gave birth to a litter of pups, she would not only clean the pups from snout to tail, she would eat the afterbirth. The reason behind this act makes a great deal of sense. Bears have a notoriously amazing sense of smell and could, without much fuss, pick up the scent of newborn wolf pups and all accompanying fluids on the wind. Cleaning the pups and eating the afterbirth diminished the chances of the pups becoming prey. So it's not much of a big leap to believe that Maya's eating poop is a remnant of her very distant past, and Maya definitely had numerous litters. Maybe, in her mind, she's always going to be a mom.

Another theory states that dogs that ingest feces are doing so because they are lacking certain vitamins or minerals in their normal diets.

I went to the doctor a couple of years ago, and he told me that my iron count was a little low. He told me to take a multivitamin. There are a multitude of options out there for dogs who need to adjust their body chemistry. Every time I catch Maya with her muzzle rooting through a clump of fresh deer pellets, the first thing that flashes through my mind is *Damn it, Maya, PetSmart has an entire* aisle *dedicated to supplements! Let's go right now and get you a fucking doggie one-a-day or something!*

And then, of course, there is the most obvious and, to our

human sensibilities, the most revolting possible reason as to why Maya eats poop: she simply likes the way it tastes.

At this very moment, in my kitchen cabinet, there are no less than four boxes of dog treats, each yummier than the next (or so Baxter has told me). Treats that most dogs go absolutely apeshit over. The cabinet is never empty. We, as a family, will sooner go without bread, eggs, and milk than suffer the unspeakable thought of the dogs not having their treats. Maya, as well as Baxter and Molly, all know exactly where the cabinet is, and they know exactly what they have to do to get one of us to give them something from the cabinet—and, trust me, it ain't much.

Maya loves these treats. In anticipation of receiving a treat she will do a little thing I like to call "the prance dance." She hops from one front paw to the other, her eyes bright and active, tail swishing like a metronome on speed. For a pile of shit she will channel Bob Fosse.

I recently came down early one morning after some insistent whimpering woke me from a deep sleep. We keep Maya and Molly in a little dog pen overnight to keep them from peeing on the furniture. Under normal circumstances Maya and Molly are jumping and pushing on the pen door to be let out in the morning. On this morning, only Molly was jumping to be released. In the still dark room I could just make out Maya, hunched over something on the floor of the pen.

"*Shit!*" I said out loud.

Shit indeed.

Under normal circumstances, Maya's a very compliant dog.

I can reach into her mouth when she's chewing on a rawhide bone and she will let me take it without any hesitation or sign of aggression. Not so with poop.

"Maya, leave it! Maya, get away! Maya, for the love of God, *you're eating shit*!!"

She looks at me with her big, soulful eyes as if to say "Uh, excuse me, do you not see that I'm right in the middle of eating Molly's crap?"

"Yes, Maya I do see that you're in the middle of eating Molly's crap…do YOU see that you're eating Molly's crap?"

I have to pick her up and take her away from the pile, locking her out of the dog pen, while I go and get the tools of the turd trade, all of which we are always well stocked: disinfectant wipes, paper towels, and ziplock bags.

My wife and I have a joke when we arrive downstairs in the morning and there is no sign of any poop in the pen:

"Looks like Molly was a good girl—no poop in the night," my wife says.

"Or Maya got hungry," I reply.

Look, I could read a hundred theories as to why Maya chooses to eat poop: it wouldn't matter. It wouldn't, pardon the expression, make that fact go down any easier. I'm as repulsed as everyone is by the thought of this. We're humans. We're supposed to be disgusted by this act. After all, that's one of those defining things on that list of things that clearly marks the border between man and beast—right? And if it isn't, then someone tell me who keeps tabs on that list, because I'm heading to that person's house right now and adding it! Animals are animals and people are people. Sure, guys always joke around how if they could lick their own testicles like a male dog can do, they would never leave the house. But, we're not really serious about that. I mean, that would just be, you know, weird and wrong and unacceptable. Right? I mean... c'mon.

What was I saying?

Right: The line between man and animal.

Look, I love Maya to pieces. She is the sweetest, gentlest dog I have ever been around. But, when she chows down and has a little "fecal-fest," love quickly, albeit temporarily, turns to total disgust.

There's an old joke about the very first person who ate a lobster, and how that person must have been beyond starving to eat such a hideous creature. This joke popped into my head after I finished my most recent doody duty.

At some point in her life Maya tried eating poop for the very first time. On the scale of willingness to try new things, shit has got to be off the damn charts, right? It certainly is on mine. But although Maya's actions are just too nasty to talk about (but obviously not too nasty to write about), there is a small, a very, very small part of me that admires her. It may have been after her first litter of puppies or on some very uneventful day, but one day—whether by choice or by instinct—Maya tried something for the first time. And, I guess, liked it.

As a child I was a very picky eater. My mom, in her efforts to have me try something beyond the pizza/cheeseburger/tuna sandwich food group, would always say, "How do you know you don't like it if you never try it?" Of course, she was right. And in later years, I did try new things. Some I hated, some I liked, and one I even fell in love with.

❦ ❦ ❦

There are plenty of people who met on the Internet. My wife and I fall into that category. We were both living in Florida at the time, my wife working in the financial aid field and me in the marketing department of a large company in Miami.

I can't speak for my wife, but as for myself, I guess you can say that I was dabbling in dating, which in my case meant going to dinner with a total stranger and after five minutes realizing that I would much rather be home reading a book. Did I date a lot? Let's just say I quickly earned a Barnes and Noble preferred customer card. Then again, I've never been much of a dater.

I've always been one of those guys who prefers the consistency and comfort that comes from being in a long-term relationship. But my first marriage had recently come to an end after becoming highly inconsistent and terribly uncomfortable. So, as my friends and family were telling me at the time, I needed to *put myself out there*. I absolutely hate that phrase. Makes it sound as if I had been in the dark part of the relationship warehouse waiting to be perched out on a shelf in the harshly lit dating supermarket.

"Attention, shoppers, we have a new addition in the recently divorced, white, Jewish aisle."

It was about as much fun as it sounds.

At about the same time that I took my place in the market, the digital age was beginning to stretch its wings. One of the results of that flight was the proliferation of websites dedicated to helping people find that next special someone.

"Matt, have you seen this website called jdate.com?" a coworker asked me.

I hadn't. Jdate? *Seriously?* So now the "chosen" people were being chosen with the click of a mouse.

"You should check it out. You've got nothing to lose, right?" *Loss of dignity immediately comes to mind.*

Let me just touch on the whole Jewish thing for a moment.

I wasn't necessarily looking for a permanent someone, let alone a Jewish permanent someone. The fact that this website happened to be for Jewish singles didn't offer any additional appeal to me, nor did it provide any additional hesitancy on my part. My first wife was Jewish. My second wife, if that ever were to happen, could be Jewish...or not. The website could have been ocdate.com for obsessive compulsives, and it wouldn't have mattered. But, let's face it, dating a fellow Jew does offer a few advantages.

The first is that if you do end up getting married, the question of what religion you are raising your kids is removed. The second is that you don't have to explain all of the Yiddish curse words. It's like religious shorthand. But, hey, as the failure of my first marriage attests to, marrying a fellow Jew guarantees nothing. For me, being Jewish is sort of like my little toe. If one day I woke up and my little toe was gone, would it really impact my life? Would it change who I am as a person? Probably not. I'd still be able to walk and exercise and go about my life without much of a difference except, of course, being highly self-conscious during sandal season. That's how I feel about being Jewish. It's a part of me, but like a little toe part. Sure, I'd like to keep it, but if I should suffer some terrible toe mishap, well, life goes on.

So one day, apparently bored to tears, I logged on to jdate .com to kill some time. And, to give you a sense of how long ago this actually was, the website was free, which was what I anticipated it would be worth to me: zip.

Recently divorced, newly single, freshly separated, ready to take on life. It began to sound like the words you see splashed on the windshields at the used car lot on Saturday afternoons:

"Mint, only one husband."

"Minor body work, but reliable."

"High mileage but runs like a top."

I wasn't *really* considering doing this, was I?

Yep, apparently I was cruising the lot and kicking the tires.

"Hey Matt, how about this one?" my coworker shouted a bit too loudly one day.

Dude, I'm not shopping for a puppy! How about *this* one?

I leaned over to look at his computer screen. She was pretty. *Really* pretty.

Hmmm, how about *this one?*

We'll do a date. No harm in that, right? Odds are she'll have some really annoying habit, or an irritating voice, and I'll be home in bed within the hour getting cozy with some historical fiction.

A kid*! Hang on a second. That changes things. I've gone from doing a tried-and-true routine that would garner solid 8s and 9s from the judges to one with several reverse twists and a risky triple backflip dismount that could easily leave me being carried off the mat by Bela Karolyi.*

A kid?

We had a first date. A really good first date. We ate and talked, and she told me about her son, and what surprised me the most was that I didn't flee the scene. It didn't bother me. Which is not to say that it didn't make me nervous; it certainly did: just not nervous enough to leave. I was willing to see how this would play out. I also had the feeling that I was falling in love.

The next thing I knew I was standing in her living room and staring down at her son, who, up until the moment before I walked through her door, was still just a concept.

I mean, I always knew he was real. I just thought that, maybe, I don't know, maybe I was holding out hope that she was just conjuring this phantom child in order to test my feelings for her; to gauge my willingness to stick around, even in the face of an impending stepchild. Nope. Not a test.

There we were, a thirty-six-year-old and a six-year-old, staring at each other like, well, a potential stepdad and stepson. It wasn't awkward. I would have *killed* for awkward. This was a level of discomfort yet to be classified by researchers holed up in some feelings think tank in Stockholm.

"Matthew, this is Matt," Melissa sweetly says, introducing her little man to me.

That's right! He has the same name as me. I totally forgot about that. That's weird. I mean, that's, that's just really odd.

It's odd, right?

I don't know. Maybe it's a sign. Do I believe in signs? I don't think so. But I believe this kid keeps looking at me. The kid with my name.

"Hi," he shyly said.

"Hey buddy," I replied while smiling.

This is too much to absorb, I told myself. *It's too...something. We had a good first date. So what? Does that mean we're meant to be together? Like, the universe is giving me a not-so-subtle hint that maybe this woman is the woman that I'm* supposed *to be with? No, I'm a realist. This is going way too fast, and I'm not going to get sucked into this whole, I don't know, whatever this situation is. Look, it was a good date, I really like her, the kid is kinda cute, he has my name, but it's been nice knowing you. Have a nice life. I'm outta here!*

I proposed while we were watching the Westminster Kennel Club dog show. I gave her my mother's ring. She said yes. We both cried a little. And a Weimaraner pooped on the green carpet at Westminster. Seriously, it did. How's that for a funny engagement story? Anyway, even though I was nowhere near Madison Square Garden on that February day, I was the big winner.

That was almost thirteen years ago, and the kid that stared at me and scared the hell out of me just graduated high school. And he's grown into a terrific person. I'm beyond lucky to have him as my stepson. And I'm blessed to have his mom for my wife. And the *only* reason I've been so incredibly happy these past thirteen years is because I tried something new. Oh, I even tried some other things.

I've tried sushi. I like it. I've tried oysters...once. I am definitely more willing to try new things the older I get, probably because the "trying new things" window gets smaller and smaller with the passage of each day. Which is why, at the end of the day, I give Maya her props. Sort of. I certainly don't condone what she chooses to try—I mean, it *is* poop. But, she's not hurting anyone by trying it, and she does seem blissfully happy while doing it. And, honestly, if you're willing to eat shit you're pretty much willing to try anything.

Even online dating.

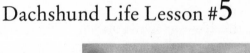

Dachshund Life Lesson #5

Try new things.
Within reason.

CHAPTER 6

The Squeaky Wheel Gets the Grease; the Whimpering Wheel Gets a Treat

You know that scene in *Shrek 2*, where Shrek and Donkey first meet Puss? The one where he stares at Shrek and Donkey with his eyes as big as saucers and welling with heavy tears? Well, Puss has nothing on Molly.

Molly is another Texas transplant. She is what's called a piebald Dachshund, because her fur is mottled black, white, and tan. She's a tiny thing, maybe twelve pounds on a really humid day.

As I already mentioned, overall Molly's a pretty happy dog. In fact, the woman we got her from used to call her "Jolly Molly" for that very reason. Nothing seems to get Molly down. Never gets too high, never gets too low. She's just a pleasant dog. Although, there is one thing that Molly does that brings *me* and anyone else within earshot down. When she wants attention, and when it suits her needs, Molly can be quite the drama queen.

I'll set the scene.

I'm sitting on the couch reading a book or watching something on TV. After several moments, I sense a presence next to me. Without glancing over I already know what's going to happen next. A small, wet nose inserts itself under my forearm and begins pushing my arm up.

I then feel her short, smooth fur brush under my arm, culminating in about fourteen inches of Dachshund sidling next to me. She's pushing against me like she wants me to give her my lunch money. I ignore her.

Molly doesn't like to be ignored.

And so, she resorts to the one thing that she excels at, other than being happy: she goes all Bambi on my ass.

She cries.

I kept all of the documents that we received when we adopted Molly, and I remember going through them pretty thoroughly, but I can't seem to recall if she ever attended the Actor's Studio or had a five-episode arc on *Days of our Lives*. This dog can turn on the waterworks like a pro. Practically on cue! But, the truth is, her true power lies not in crying, but in *preventing* herself from crying.

The one thing sadder than seeing someone cry is seeing someone on the *verge* of crying.

The quivering lower lip, the flush in the cheeks, eyes pregnant with buckets of salty sentiment ready to sodden the first available shoulder. Crying is sad; *almost* crying is painful.

I look at her. Her huge, doelike eyes stare at me, the perfect amount of moisture perched precariously on the rim of her lower eyelid adding just the right touch of *pathetique*.

She doesn't blink. This dog does not blink!

She's a freak.

I'm not kidding.

She stares, the wetness builds. I stare, her whiskers tremble. She's the Meryl Streep of her generation, or at the very least, her litter. I remain unmoved.

They're not real tears!

She's not actually crying!

I'm being ridiculous. She's a dog!

And then—cue the SFX—the whimpering begins.

They start off more as a very soft vibration, like a Sonicare toothbrush that's almost out of battery power. You don't hear her whimpers as much as feel them. Apparently, at some point in her past, Molly crossed paths with George Lucas, because what's going on in her body, and in my ears, is at a quality and magnitude that surely involves the talented folks at Industrial Light and Magic.

No response from Daddy.

So, she goes sonic.

My back molars start to hurt and my eyes wince. A crystal flower vase begins to tremble ever so slightly. Somewhere in the Arctic Ocean, beluga whales are having hissy fits. I know she's sitting right next to me, safe as can be, but she sounds as if Laurence Olivier is peppering her with the same question over and over:

Is it safe…to leave you home alone and not put you in your crate?

Chilling. Truly chilling.

I know what she's doing. It's nothing new. She just wants

something. Perhaps to go outside, where she will do nothing but lay in the driveway. Or maybe she's angling for a treat, which she will inhale and, ultimately, act as nothing more than a whining intermezzo. Or she's whining because she wants attention. Those are the possibilities in their entirety; Molly has a short menu.

Don't give in, Matt.

Hmmmmmmm–hmmmmmMMMMMMMMM!

"Molly, *stop it*!"

Eyes welling, welling, welling…

Keith Moon is doing a solo on my eardrums.

Matt, don't… *don't*…

🦴 🦴 🦴

So we go outside.

Turns out it was the "lying in the driveway" whine. Shocking. I think she's actually smiling.

What can I say: I am but a mortal man.

And more than a little jealous.

When Molly wants something she uses everything in her arsenal to get it. Me? I sit there waiting for the cosmos to bring things to me. I guess there's something to be said for saying something.

Not that I would know.

🦴 🦴 🦴

I can't say for certain, given the passage of time and the failing memory that goes with it, but I can't seem to recall ever being told to shut up.

I don't mean in conversation. Of course, I've had my share of *Dude, shut the fuck up* and *Be quiet, you don't know what you're talking about.* What I mean is that nobody has ever told me to shut up because I was simply talking too much.

I'm not a mute. I'm not an Ellen Jamesian from *The World According to Garp*, with a little pad and pencil hanging from my neck on which I frantically scribble, trying to keep up with my mind. It's just that given the choice, I prefer listening to speaking. I'm in good company.

Thomas Jefferson was notorious for saying little in the way of conversation or commentary. Turns out he was a bit more comfortable with the old quill and ink. Safe to say he got his points across rather well, wouldn't you agree? The Godfather wasn't much of a great conversationalist, and yet through coercion, intimidation, and the odd assassination or two, he let people know what he was thinking. You gotta problem with that? I didn't think so.

I speak when I have something to say, and when I'm done I stop speaking. I'm pretty sure that's how it's supposed to work. What's really sad is that I come into contact with far too many people who don't seem to have any issues with continuing to speak long after they have anything of interest to say.

"Oh, well, that's just Matt, he doesn't talk much" is a pretty common comment on my silence.

But I'm fine with it. It's just the way I am, which is not to say that my lack of verbosity hasn't come back to bite me in the ass on more than one occasion.

If nice guys finish last, then guys who choose not to talk

a lot finish just a few scant paces ahead of the nice guys. But hey, at least I'm not one of *those* losers, right?

I've been in many situations, particularly in my career, where I should have said something, should have made my position known, but didn't. Times when I knew that the general consensus wasn't my consensus, but chose to simply go with the rest of the herd. And, I've had moments where I should have tooted my own horn, assumed someone else would toot it for me, and was left totally tootless.

I don't like confrontation. I'm sure that's been a big part of it. If you don't say anything, then nobody can debate you on it, and if you don't debate you can't lose that debate. I guess I've always felt that in time, things would always work themselves out; that I would at some point get the recognition I was due. For the most part, I'm still waiting.

Things changed for me—well, *I* changed for me, when I was nineteen. And, as with so many moments of change, it was a change born from a death.

My dad was not what you would call a wallflower. Born and raised in Brooklyn, my dad had a personality as big as the borough he called home. He was boisterous and engaging, fun and friendly, and, as most dads seem to be in their child's memories, afraid of nothing.

Which is to say he was nothing like me.

Shortly after we moved to Long Island when I was around twelve, I joined a local football league. The team used to practice on a large field that separated the grammar school from the high school. And, on one side of that field were a row of houses. One of those houses was mine. And, on the other side of the fence that ran the length of that field, through every practice, was my dad. Through every sprint, pass, and huddle he would stand there, smoking his cigarettes, exhorting me through my drills. And with every "Atta boy, Matty" I would want to seep into the cleat-churned grass and disappear.

"Uh, Dad, can you *please* not yell so loud?" I would plead.

I told him that it was breaking my concentration, when in reality it was breaking my will to live. I was beyond embarrassed. I felt like a spotlight was being shined upon me, emphasizing every block I missed and every ragged breath I drew. In other words, I was trying my best to do what every twelve-year-old boy tries to do when among other twelve-year-old boys: not stand out. And here was this loud, and I mean *really* loud guy, not more than fifty feet away from me, doing everything in his power to the contrary.

How can he be my dad? I'd often wonder. *We're nothing alike.*

Perhaps there was a mix-up at the hospital and my dad, in reality, was a quiet, somewhat bookish British expat whose idea of a good time was sequestering himself in a wood-paneled library, in front of a crackling fire, while thumbing through a first edition of *Finnegans Wake*.

Alas, my birth certificate and my mother's undying defense of the fine, dedicated folks in the maternity ward at Maimonides Hospital, in Brooklyn, New York, proved fairly conclusively that this was not the case. Apparently, the lunatic on the other side of the fence was mine.

But only until I was nineteen.

❦ ❦ ❦

My family had recently relocated to Los Angeles, after my parents purchased an automotive repair franchise in Hollywood, in an attempt to give their three sons a better, sun-kissed, palm-tree-lined life.

We absolutely hated it.

We hated that it felt foreign. We hated that our friends were now three thousand miles away. My brothers hated being the new kids in school, and I hated trying to maintain a relationship with my girlfriend over the phone, a relationship that ended only a couple of months after we moved into a three-bedroom apartment in Sherman Oaks, a suburb of Los Angeles.

I have a very vivid memory of lying in one of those bedrooms one night, pining away for my now ex-girlfriend, listening to a local FM station that featured a heavy rotation of Steely Dan, the Eagles, and Fleetwood Mac. I even remember the exact date, but not because I have some remarkable ability to remember dates. *Most* people my age remember that date; *many* people remember that date. December 8, 1980.

The music abruptly faded out, and the DJ came on to somberly announce that John Lennon had been shot and killed outside the Dakota apartment building in New York City.

Up to that point in my life, I experienced the odd moment

of sadness, but that night, in that awful bedroom, hearing that terrible news, sadness proceeded to bend me into a fetal ball of temper and tears.

It wasn't very long after that awful night that we all agreed that California wasn't for us and we would go back home. All except one.

My dad loved California. He took to it like a native. He marveled at the weather, the friendliness of the people, but mostly the opportunity it was affording him to provide a better life for his family. And he couldn't understand how anyone could not, as Randy Newman sang at the time, "love L.A." But we didn't. After much discussion between my parents, it was decided that we would sell the automotive shop, move back to New York, and start over. My mom, brothers, and I were ecstatic; my dad was resigned.

The plan was that we would all move back home, except for my dad, who would remain behind to sell the shop, and then join us in New York. My mom quickly found an apartment in a two-family house back in our hometown of Valley Stream. My brothers started school again, and I debated whether or not to enroll in a local community college. The truth was, I wasn't sure what I wanted to do with myself. The whole California situation left me pretty rattled and unsure what path my life would or should take. Fortunately, the college decided for me. I missed the cutoff date to enroll, which left me with nothing but time on my hands and no productive way in which to fill it. My mom suggested that since I wasn't going to school that semester, maybe I should go out to Los Angeles to keep my father company while he was trying to sell the shop. I said that as long as it was temporary, I would go. Besides, I missed my father.

My dad had moved into a studio apartment that was close to the shop, which was located at the intersection of Melrose and Vine, a redheaded stepchild to the more famous intersection of Hollywood and Vine. I spent a lot of time in the tiny apartment, watching bad daytime TV and talking on the phone with my mom, keeping her informed of my dad's efforts to get the both of us back home where we belonged. One day, in March 1981, the phone rang. I assumed it was my mother checking in.

"Hi, is this Matt Ziselman?" a serious-toned adult asked.

"Yes, who's this?"

"Matt, my name is Dr. F. I work at Kaiser Foundation Hospital. Your father was brought into the hospital about fifteen minutes ago, complaining of chest pains and shortness of breath. He told us to call this number and speak to you. Uh, Matt, is your mom there? Can I speak to *her*?"

Not now. Please, not here.

"My mom's in New York. Is he going to be okay? What happened to him?"

"Matt, do you have a car? Do you drive?"

"My dad has the car. Had the car."

Mom.

"Okay, do you have someone, a relative, that can drive you here?"

"I can ask my uncle Bill. I can call him."

"Okay, Matt, that sounds good. It's Kaiser Foundation on Sunset Boulevard. Again, my name is Dr. F. Did you write all that down? Go to the emergency room, ask for me, and I'll come get you. Okay? Do you understand?"

"I do. I'm going to call my uncle and we'll be right down."

"Okay, Matt."

"Is he okay? Is he going to be okay?"

"Matt, hang up and call your uncle."

I don't actually remember calling my uncle or getting to the hospital. My memory abruptly picks up again in a room filled with three things: people, machines, and my father.

"Matt?"

"Mhmm."

"Matt? Are you all right?"

I managed a nod as I stared at the scene in front of me, where the only person not moving was my father. The air was peppered with requests and demands.

I want to start a line into the femoral, please. What's his respiration?

"Matt, your dad has had a heart attack. Right now, we're doing everything we can to stabilize him. Does your dad smoke?"

"Yes."

"Okay."

Can someone please give me a blood ox level?

"Do you know if he's on any medication?"

"I dunno."

He leaned away from me and whispered something into a nurse's ear.

"Matt, where's your uncle?"

"He's outside parking the car. He's coming. What's happening?"

"Matt," he began, while gently pulling me just outside the door of the room. "We're doing our best to help your father, but he's very sick. I want you to listen very carefully to what I'm going to say to you, okay? Your dad is still conscious; he's still able to communicate with us. I would like your dad to speak to your mom."

"She's in New York."

Beep—beep—beep—beep—beep—

"I know. We can call her right now and put her on the phone with your dad."

"Is that so she can tell you that it's okay to do whatever you need to do to help him? Because I can tell you right now that—"

He interrupted me by placing his hand on my shoulder.

"Matt," he said in a softer, steady tone, "I want them to talk to each other."

He stopped speaking but kept looking at me. He was waiting for me to take in what he'd just said.

"Is he going to die?" I managed to coax from my clenching throat.

"Matt, your father is very sick. I don't know if he's going to make it through the night. I want him to hear your mom; I want your mom to hear him. Do you understand what I'm saying?"

I paused a moment to admit to myself that I understood. "Yeah."

"Would you like me to talk to her first?"

"No, I'll do it."

"Okay, come over here."

He guided me between the bodies and machines that were now keeping my father's life from leaving him. I arrived at a small, bedside table with a phone on it.

"Press 9 first, and then dial your mom's number, okay?"

The noise in the room dropped several respectful decibels so all I heard were the various sounds of the different machines. I reached for the phone receiver with my right hand and cradled it between my right ear and right shoulder. As I began to dial the number and prepare to break my mother's heart, my left hand was suddenly filled with another. I looked at my dad's hand in mine. My eyes tracked past the tubes and wires that dotted and assaulted his arm, shoulder, and chest. My gaze eventually arrived at his face, where I found his eyes locked onto mine. They were wet and pleading. I offered a trembling smile. His lips moved. With the receiver still pressed to my right ear, I leaned in and put my left ear next to his mouth where, in a tremulous whisper, I heard, "Okay. Don't be scared. Love you. Going to be okay."

"Hello," my mom said on the fifth ring.

My hand never left his.

❧ ❧ ❧

My mom flew out to be with him during his recovery. A week passed. Early one morning, she answered the phone and was told that he had died an hour earlier.

I suppose it's natural, when you experience something like that, for your mind to rewind through the past years: the times you've had, the people you had them with. I thought a lot about my dad in the weeks and months that followed. And it was amazing how his loudness suddenly didn't seem so loud. How his antics on the other side of the fence and in the bleachers on game day stopped being antics and became a father's pride writ large for all to see. After he was gone none of it seemed as embarrassing as it once did. And that changed me.

Right or wrong, I came to the conclusion that my dad was the way he was for two reasons. The first was that it was just his personality. Some people are just born bigger than others. People whose personalities cannot be contained by the barrier of their bones or the cover of their skins. Their life force overflows their borders.

The second reason was that the world demands it.

Let's face it: the world has neither the patience nor the inclination to listen to those who whisper. To those, who expect to be recognized simply by showing up. Woody Allen even once famously said that 80 percent of success is just showing up. I think the other 20 percent is making your presence known once you do. My dad was a 20 percent man.

Not too long after my dad died, I began to notice a gradual change in myself.

I started to chime in more on conversations. I began offering unsolicited opinions. I started listening to what was being said around me, and if I didn't like what I was hearing, or I disagreed with what I was hearing, I let people know about it. In ways, both large and small, I started to make my feelings known. And one of the first things I felt was this:

I was not born my father's son.

But in my nineteenth year I think I *became* my father's son.

I'm still speaking up. In fact, this book is a form of me speaking up. And while speaking up and making my presence known doesn't always result in anything even close to a golden ticket, I feel better for having said something. I feel better for being heard.

So, as it turns out, Jolly Molly has the right idea. Try as I might, I can't ignore her. She won't hear of it. And so the chin trembles, the eyes moisten, and the tears hang suspended on the lower rim of a Bambi-shaped eye. Hey, it works for her. Stick with your strengths, I say. Personally, tears aren't my things. Let's face it: I don't really have the cheekbones for optimal tear flow. But, fear not. If I want your attention I'll get it. If I have something to say you'll know it. After all, I *am* my father's son.

Dachshund Life Lesson #6

Be heard.

CHAPTER 7

You Lick Your *Human* with That Tongue?

I bathe in the morning.

Well, actually, I *get* bathed in the morning.

Upon awakening I take my place in a chair by the living room window and it is there, drenched in the first blush of morning, that I also get drenched with copious amounts of saliva, courtesy of Baxter. And I'm not talking about soft gentle passes with a slightly dampened tongue. I'm talking about something that's closer to abuse than affection. In fact, I'm not even sure if it has *anything* to do with affection.

In my mind I'm thinking, *Look how much this dog loves me. Can I really be that awesome?* In Baxter's mind it's probably closer to *How lucky am I to have this salt lick delivered to me every morning? The service here really is exceptional.*

Emmy often gets mad at me because I say hello to Baxter first every morning. I do my best to explain to her that I really don't have much of a say in the matter. He will follow my every move until I sit myself down and offer up my face for his amusement.

"But Daddy, *I'm your daughter*!" she protests.

"Emmy, do you see what he does? Daddy's not participating—Daddy's a hostage! A prop! Just let him finish, and then I'll come say good morning."

Let him finish.

I can't even believe I say that, but I do. And it's true. Baxter is just one of those dogs—one of those Dachshunds; the more I try to push him away, the harder he's going to push back. So I figure I'll let him do his thing and then I can get on with my day. Most Dachshund owners will say the same thing that I'm about to say: you have to pick your battles so you can live to fight and, let's face it, probably lose another day.

Reeking of kibble and who knows what else.

Experts who know about such things say that a Komodo dragon has the most bacteria-ridden mouth in the animal kingdom, which is an interesting fact, rivaled *only* by another interesting fact—namely, that there are people whose field of study is the mouth of an oversized lizard with poor oral hygiene. Growing up, I remember, I was constantly hearing how a dog's saliva is very clean. It probably is when compared to, say, the alpha predator on Komodo Island? I don't know about a dog's saliva being clean or not. All I know is that Baxter's breath is no picnic. But it is, by far, the least offensive of any of the dogs' breath.

Molly's breath is a bit harder on the senses. Fortunately, though, she does not have the same licking procedure as Baxter. When I put my face close to hers, she is more than happy to oblige. Molly employs what I call the cobra approach. She bobs and weaves her little pointy nose and then, right when you think she's not going to oblige with lightning-fast speed, she darts in and usually catches me on my teeth. She pecks. She's like a pissed-off chicken. Her licks are closer to injection than affection. When I allow Molly to lick my face I know that to a certain degree I'm risking physical harm. But she's so damn cute, what's a couple of minor abrasions or a bruised cornea, right?

Maya wins, though. Maya's breath is the foulest of the foul, the rankest of the rank. It smells like . . . I don't even know if I can put it into words. Some things you just have to experience, not that I would want you to experience it—after all, you were kind enough to buy this book. Let me see if I can capture the funk going on in Maya's mouth without putting you in any danger.

Pretend you're walking along the beach and you come upon a dead animal of some kind. Not a mouse. Not a raccoon. Something more substantial, like a goat. Let's not get into the whole "why is there a goat on the beach discussion." Just work with me here, okay?

You find a goat on the beach that has obviously been dead for at least a couple of weeks, and during those couple of weeks, there has been a freakish heat wave with temperatures every day in the nineties. Oh, and you happen upon this dead goat at low tide. That begins to give you a sense of Maya's breath.

Just barely.

Part of it is age: she is nine, and it's not uncommon for older dogs to develop bad breath. I think a lot of it also stems from the years of neglect she endured before she came to live with us. And, of course, there's her occasional foray into all things fecal that, no matter how many Tic Tacs you eat, tend to linger on the palate. If you were to get within a few inches of her face you would understand what I'm talking about. The thing is, you would never get within a few inches of Maya's face. Because Maya does not lick. Maya does not douse me in canine cologne. The only bathing Maya is involved with are the ones that we give her every month.

It is truly a special moment when Maya quietly, and hesitantly, touches my nose with her tongue. It's not even a proper lick, really; it's a tap. And it's more likely to be my hand. It's so subtle and so infrequent that it barely qualifies as a gesture, but it means the absolute world to me. That little gesture, contrary to appearances, is pretty damn big.

🦴 🦴 🦴 .

I'm full of excuses:

I don't have time, I'm too busy, I'm not in the mood (shocking), let's see what tomorrow brings, I'm reading, I'm watching something, I have to clean up Molly's crap, I'm finishing an e-mail, I have to take out the garbage, I have to get up early, I got in too late, I have to catch a plane, I'm *so* not in the mood, I'm too tired, and, of course, we'll see. And that's just the beginning. I would write some more, but I'm right in the middle of writing something else, so I'll have to get back to you with some more excuses.

I'm full of them.

The excuses pile up oh so fast, creating an often-insurmountable mountain of wasted moments and missed opportunities. I tend to blame it on life in general. It's out of

my control. Don't blame me for this runaway train of obliga-
tions I'm barely hanging on to as it screams down the track
that will never end until *I* end.

I do my best to listen and watch. I try my mightiest to pay
attention to those moments that my wife tells me are worth
paying attention to. I focus and force myself, and yet I leave a
trail of disappointment and frowns in my wake. It bothers me.
It hurts me to think that I'm hurting the ones I love by not
showing that love in thirty seconds of undivided attention, or a
hug that lasts longer than it takes to *spell* the word *hug*.

Emily does this thing before she goes to bed. Essentially, it's
an excruciatingly long, somewhat complex bedtime routine
that, appropriately enough, has come to be known as "the
Routine."

It's this weird amalgam of movie quotes, calls-and-
responses, and "Don't let the bedbugs bite." Probably best if
you don't try to wrap your head around it; it's a kid thing—
need I say more? You're probably thinking, *That's so sweet.* I
thought it was sweet, too...the first couple of hundred times.
The Routine has been going on now for about two years. It
occurs when my wife and I are at our most tired and mentally
drained. In other words, it occurs when my patience is at its
breaking point and my excuses are at their towering limit.

"Emmy, can we please skip the Routine tonight? My brain
is fried."

"But Daddyyyyyyyyyy..."

It's that pleading, plaintive whine that daddys the world over are all too familiar with, in such contexts as:

"But Daddyyyyy, you said we could gooooo..."

"Daddyyyyyy, you promised..."

"Pleeeease, Daddyyyyyy, Mommy said it was okay..."

And, like *daddyyyyys* everywhere, I cave like a guy who just wants to get some sleep.

Because the only thing standing between me and oh-so-sweet slumber is the Routine, so the quicker we do it the sooner I'm sawing some serious wood. The problem is that the Routine is not quick. You know what's quick? Midday traffic in Manhattan. Know what else is quick? High Mass. At the Vatican. On Christmas Eve.

It begins with Emily giving Melissa and I a specific amount of kisses in a very specific sequence. This includes kisses both on the face and on the forehead. If either we or Emmy messes up the sequence, we must start over from the beginning. It's like a cruel board game from Parker Brothers that involves sleep deprivation and psychotic episodes. And all of the game pieces are shaped like little Ambien: *Sleepy Land*. The Routine also involves what can best be described as a combination of hugs and nuzzling... *huzzles*. But it is the kisses that rule. Screw those up and it's a long night. Then, of course, there's the dialogue.

"Will you check on me?" she asks both my wife and me.

"Yes," we respond in unison.

"Love you," she proclaims.

"Love *you*," we singsong in response.

"G'night."

"Good *night*!"

"Sleep well, you guys."

"You too Bobo," we answer with one of the sixteen nicknames we have for her.

And that's pretty much the Routine.

Sometimes.

It's not unusual at all for five or ten minutes to pass, my wife fast asleep, myself deeply immersed in whatever book is currently on my night table when, out of the darkened silence comes a loud:

"G'NIGHT, DADDY!"

Jesus Christ!

"Good *night, Emmy*! Go to *sleep*!"

After my heart reverts back to normal sinus rhythm, I'm able to get back into the book I'm reading, and another Routine *truly* comes to an end.

🦴 🦴 🦴

Melissa and I have asked ourselves how long we should allow the Routine to go on. Emmy is coming up on eleven. It seems like it should have stopped, or we should have put a stop to it, a couple of years ago. We have broached the subject with Emmy on more than one occasion, and her response is usually something to the effect of:

"But I love you guys, and it helps me fall asleep knowing that *you* love *me*."

That's usually the place where the conversation about ending the Routine comes to its *own* end.

During one of these conversations my wife said something that not only put an end to Routine-ending talk, at least for a while, but also shined a very bright light on a sad and all-too-frequent example of my inability to find the time to appreciate what's important.

"I know it's exhausting, you're tired, I'm tired, but, one day she's going to stop doing the Routine, and then at some point in the future you and I are going to be laying in our bed saying, 'Hey, remember when Emmy used to do the Routine?' and we're going to wish that she still did."

My wife has that wonderful ability to make the perfect point while simultaneously bringing me to tears.

🦴 🦴 🦴

Of course, we still complain to each other about the Routine. We struggle to keep our eyes open while trying to keep track of how many kisses Mommy got and reciting that line from *SpongeBob SquarePants* that never fails to make Emmy giggle.

We do our little call-and-response with as much enthusiasm as we can muster, and I do my very best to try not to let her latent *G'nights* interrupt my nightly reading—or my blood from flowing in its predetermined course.

We do this because that night—the night where there will be no little girl bestowing kisses—is rapidly approaching. It probably won't be tonight, but it's out there. A few silly kisses? Thirty seconds of tender wishes? Pretty small in the scheme of things. But I guess that's what makes it so big.

🦴 🦴 🦴

Bad breath and all, Maya has taught me that little things matter. The things we don't think twice about, the things that don't give us a moment's pause, but probably should. *Definitely* should.

Things that are so much more than what they appear to be on the surface. A fleeting touch of a tongue from a dog with hellish halitosis will pass without any fanfare. But what I've come to realize is this: That's not just a touch. It's a wink. Because Maya knows that *I* know.

Or at least, I know *now*.

And that, my friends—like a kiss in the dark from a little girl—is all that matters.

Dachshund Life Lesson #7

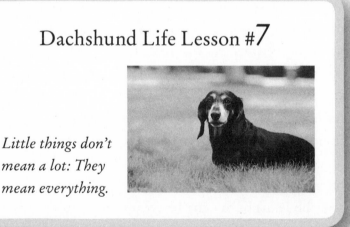

Little things don't mean a lot: They mean everything.

CHAPTER **8**

Urine My World Now

Every month I pay landscapers a sizable amount of money to tend to my lawn. They mow it, edge it, weed it, fertilize it, and generally show it the kind of attention usually reserved for newborns. And I have no doubt at all that I am throwing my money down the toilet. Because, while the landscaper bills come to *me*, my front lawn has gone, in the truest sense of the phrase, to the dogs.

While Baxter just turned five, his bladder seems to be stuck in the "terrible twos," because with every release of his urine I can hear the not-so-subtle refrain of *mine, mine, mine!* He's not urinating—*he's claiming.*

Okay, this section over here is mine. This part next to the Japanese maple, mine. Oh, hey, Matt, you see that part over there, where the gardener seeded like, I don't know, maybe a month ago? THAT'S MINE, TOO!

His canine incontinence is leaving a sad trail of yellow patches across what was, for a brief, shining moment, a swath of enviable green.

Of course, Baxter isn't the only one to soil my soil. Maya and Molly are just as guilty in reaping what they sow...or shitting what they eat, however you want to put it. Maya will take a few quiet moments, find just the right spot, and do her business. Molly, apparently on an endless search for either the lost treasure of El Dorado or Amelia Earhart, will wander and wander before answering the long-distance call of nature. I'm serious. When I come back into the house after taking Molly outside, I have visibly aged. And even though the girls use and abuse the front yard just as much as Baxter, I think Baxter just relishes it more. It's as if he knows how much it pains me to see him pee all over the landscaper's hard work and my hard-earned money, and that gives him some kind of sick thrill. Look, I don't have a degree in theology or any research to back me up on this, but I have a gut feeling that Baxter just may be the Devil. Not a minor demon, mind you, the Devil! I'm seriously considering dousing him with holy water, while I intone, "The power of crabgrass compels you! The power of crabgrass compels you!"

I'll sometimes take Baxter out very early in the morning. The sun has just risen. It's serenely quiet. A bird tweets in the distance. It's one of those mornings you see portrayed in a Folger's coffee commercial, except instead of hearing the comforting drip of that glorious first cup of joe, I hear the unmistakable sound of a hot stream of urine forcefully splattering against the hard-packed earth. As it steams in the morning chill Baxter slowly turns his head around (thankfully, not *all* the way around) and looks me right in the eye. He holds my gaze.

That little bastard!

After a solid forty-five seconds has elapsed, he straightens his head and slowly walks away from the sodden patch of grass, with a smug look of self-satisfaction on his face.

Sigh.

A swath of green. You really should have seen it.

🦴 🦴 🦴

I've said this to my wife on more than one occasion: for all of his frustrating behavior and all of the times I've seriously wondered if he was worth the hassle, I have a tremendous amount of respect for Baxter. Yes, he annoys me on a daily basis, but the more time I've spent with him and watched him, he definitely has certain qualities that serve him well. While I understand that urinating on the ground isn't technically a quality, nor all that difficult to achieve, it's the manner in which he goes about it that I sort of appreciate. He's marking his territory, a message for all of the other dogs in the neighborhood, something to the effect of *If I even see a hind leg look like it's getting ready to be cocked, you are in for a big bowl of hurt.* I get it. He's simply doing something that any dog does, regardless of breed or temperament. But in much the same way that every dog owner will look at their dog and think that maybe there's something more going on behind those eyes, I look at Baxter's marking as more than simply him saying, *This belongs to me*—he's saying, *This is what I do.*

🦴 🦴 🦴

I wish I had something, *anything*, that I enjoyed to do as much as Baxter seems to enjoy peeing and marking his territory (aka my front yard). I love reading, but that doesn't really require much more than some good light and a book for me to boldly proclaim, "I'm going to read for a while." I open the book, I start to read, and people pretty much leave me alone because, you know, they see me reading. So, yeah, reading...not much need for marking that territory.

Now that I think about it, I guess I lead a rather dull, uneventful life. But, obviously I like it uneventful, if I didn't I'd fill it with more events. I mean, if I ever feel the need to jump out of a plane (I won't) or go cage-diving with great white sharks (see previous parenthetical statement) I can. But, on the whole, I just don't get that excited over things. And certainly nothing worth peeing over.

Except for writing.

Let me be clear. I'm not saying in any way that what I write is *worth* peeing over, so you're not under any kind of obligation. I'm talking about the act, the process of writing. I love it! I love decluttering my desk in preparation for the explosion of creativity that is sure to follow, which, oddly enough, often looks a lot like I'm staring at the wall—but, trust me, that's creativity at its finest. There's an old saying that says that writing is the only job where staring out a window is considered working. I'll buy that.

I like dimming the lights, selecting just the right white noise to inspire me. Maybe some Tibetan wind chimes or humpback whales in a particularly randy mood. And then the short, staccato clicks of my laptop keys as my fingers fly across the board, trying desperately to keep pace with the thoughts racing through my mind. Although, as I write these *particular* words, it sounds more like a pair of drunken Manolo Blahniks walking down a morgue hallway at 2:00 a.m. Not much clattering going on right now. Nope. Not. A. Whole. Lot.

But it's the silence between the clicks where the rush comes from. That's where everything is fair game. The magic, the opportunity, the line that's going to stay with me after I hit Save for the night, are in that silence. I want to make noise. I want to take that nice white piece of paper and make it absolutely filthy. I love that. I've loved it for quite some time.

I think a great many writers begin life as readers. And I have always read. I've always found comfort, knowledge, wisdom, entertainment, and the world at large between those two hard covers. So I don't necessarily think it's much of a surprise when a reader makes the leap to writer. On the other hand, I think it's a massive, Evel Knievel–like leap to become a *good* writer. And, if there's one thing I hate, it's heights.

🦴 🦴 🦴

My first real effort to do any kind of substantial writing (at least I thought it was substantial) was when I cowrote a horrifically bad play for a one-act play contest in high school. It was called "Like a Dummy Going over a Waterfall." I'll leave you to imagine the depths of just how bad that play must have been simply based on that title. Although, the experience wasn't all bad. I also acted in the play, winning a best-supporting actor award for my efforts. But the rush of winning was quickly tempered when, a short half hour after my triumph, I was toting our garbage cans to the curb for pickup. Thanks for snuffing out that buzz, Dad.

I wrote wonderful book reports and essays and presentations

that went over quite well, but nothing to match my theatrical triumph. I graduated high school, seriously toyed with the idea of actually pursuing an acting career, dropped out of school, put away my Oscar speech, and took a job in Manhattan as an account coordinator for a recruitment advertising company. My writing aspirations were placed in a cardboard box right next to my already tarnishing "Best Supporting Actor" plaque. I did what many writers do at one time or another: I stopped writing. But, perhaps even worse than not writing was that I stopped believing that I *could* write. And I did that for many years.

I worked, I changed jobs, I commuted, I bitched and moaned about not being fulfilled, I made very little money, I complained about being just another rat in the rat race. And I didn't write a thing. Not even for the fun that writing always used to give me. I got married, moved to Florida, struggled to find a job, watched my marriage crash and burn, and suddenly found myself wifeless, jobless, and more or less hopeless. Clearly, something had to seriously change. And it began with me telling a lie.

🦴 🦴 🦴

I had applied for a job that had "writer" as part of its title. Good enough for me! It was for a marketing company in Miami. One day I received a call from a person in Human Resources because she needed to confirm certain things on my résumé—namely, the year I graduated from college, which I had neglected to include.

"Nineteen eighty-four," I told her.

"Well Matt, it says here on your résumé that in 1984 you were working full-time in a nightclub, so how could you have graduated at the same time that you were working *full-time* at a nightclub?"

"Uh…"

"Matt, did you graduate from college?" she asked, already knowing what I would say.

Fuck!

"I didn't."

"So why did you lie?"

And so, I told her the truth: "Because I want this job so badly that I was willing to do something incredibly stupid to get it. I'm sorry, but, I just…I just really want this job, and I thought if you knew that I never graduated there's no way you'd give me a chance."

A couple of silent moments passed. And then, a sigh on the other end of the phone.

"Matt, we're going to give you a chance because I think you'll do a great job, but let me ask you one final time: is there anything else on your résumé that isn't true?"

"Nothing!"

"Then I'll see you next Monday."

And she did.

And that was my very first job where I was being paid to write. Sure, it was marketing brochures and fact sheets and all kinds of materials that don't exactly qualify as literature, but I was being compensated to put words into sentences, sentences into paragraphs, and paragraphs into cohesive thoughts. Last time I checked, that was writing. I was, in a word, happy.

Well, happier.

☙ ❧ ☙

That was about fourteen years ago. Since then, I've changed jobs a few times, climbed a couple of rungs on a sometimes rickety career ladder, and started writing things that were a bit more challenging and a bit more fulfilling. But over that time I never did a single thing to really nurture my dream of becoming a writer of books rather than brochures. I'm sure fear had a lot to do with it. Thinking of writing a book is a scary-ass thing. It's daunting. But, appropriately enough, it was a book that finally made me take action, that made me finally do something to put a flame under my ass and put some effort into making my dream real. I was finally marking my territory, and it was more like a few hesitant drips rather than a rushing torrent... but hey, marking is marking.

☙ ❧ ☙

Writing retreat. I know, it sounded a little too...crispy-crunchy to me, too. I'm thinking a circle of people standing around a fire sharing their innermost literary fears and desires, all while some pan flute music wafts on the breeze. Never was I so happy to be wrong. It was about twelve people sitting around a table telling total strangers why they considered themselves writers. Okay, I'll admit, it did take place in a charming B&B in Saugatuck, Michigan, and there might have been a lit candle or two at some point, but it was totally cool. And I so didn't think it would be.

I don't do retreats. I don't do casual gatherings. I don't do the whole "Hey, there's a total stranger; I think I'll go strike up some inane conversation about absolutely nothing" thing. I go out of my way to avoid chitchat; the way germaphobes avoid shaking hands. Walk up to a total stranger and introduce myself? Probably not going to happen. Mingling? Not so much. Yes, I schmooze for work, but that's schmoozing for dollars, totally different. There wasn't a single potential aspect to this retreat thing that appealed to me. Scratch that—there was *one*: Wade Rouse.

I had recently read Wade's wonderfully funny, sincerely shared story of how he followed *his* dream to become a full-time writer, *At Least in the City Someone Would Hear Me Scream*. It will come as no big surprise that his story resonated with me big-time. Yes, Wade was gay, and he was born and raised in rural Missouri, while I am a straight, married Jewish guy who was born in Brooklyn and grew up on Long Island, but none of that mattered because we had something in common: he had the life I wanted. No, I didn't desire to be a gay man with a flawless fashion sense and a significant, bordering-on-unhealthy obsession with Barbie dolls. He wrote what was in his heart and not what was in a creative brief, and that was what I wanted to do. In my eyes, Wade's journey seemed almost heroic. And who doesn't want to meet a hero?

So after finishing his book, I dropped him a line just to tell him how much I enjoyed it, and that was when he mentioned the writer's retreat. I debated with myself. A lot. It was expensive. It was so not my cup of tea. But I felt that I deserved to finally do this for myself. It definitely felt like a now-or-never moment. So in order to make myself more comfortable with the notion of calling myself a real writer, I would have to make myself really *un*comfortable around other people who called themselves writers, too. I owed it to my dream. So I went. I went to Saugatuck with only a few pages of writing (actually, the first five pages of what would become this book) and a suitcase full of doubt.

He was on the short side, quite thin, and lacking any kind of glowing aura that would mark him as a published author. He was very polite and totally friendly, and as far as first impressions go, he made a good one. Gradually the other attendees arrived bearing awkward hellos and armed with varied reasons they decided to attend. And I was surprised to see that people came from more than just the local area: Nebraska, Ohio, Texas, and New Jersey were all represented. Apparently, the dream of writing a book knows no boundaries—neither figuratively nor geographically—although in my case, it did require an inconvenient layover in Chicago.

Over the next three days we shared our stories, both the ones we were living and the ones we were writing. We did some writing exercises. Wade talked; we listened. We ate and wrote and talked more about writing. And our fears. On more than one occasion I thought to myself *These are my people. They get it. They know what I'm feeling because they're feeling it, too.* That made me relax. But it also made me tense because some of them were natural writers. I could hear their confidence in their words. It was the kind of confidence that made me doubt my own. When it was my turn to read, would I give anyone reason to doubt *themselves*? It was sort of mean to think that. I felt bad about thinking that...but not bad enough to *stop* thinking that.

"Okay Matt, you're the last one," Wade announced.

I had never read anything I wrote—*really* wrote—to anyone, let alone twelve total strangers. *And a published author.* I cleared my throat and took a moment to find my "happy place"—which, at that moment, was anywhere but in a sunroom in a B&B in Saugatuck, Michigan.

I began to read.

I know I could not have been reading for more than three minutes. In fact, I probably had the shortest piece out of everyone. But it felt like I had read for a day. I saw the last couple of lines before my eyes, looming like the final inverted loop on a roller coaster. The end was near. Relief was in sight. At this point I didn't even care whether or not anyone liked what I was reading, I just wanted to finish.

And I did.

I wanted applause. I wanted people to rise to their feet and shower me with adulation. That's not what happened. I got silence.

The very best kind.

Three, maybe four solid seconds of silence. And, before anyone said anything, I knew it would be okay.

"Wow, okay, *first*, it's obvious you can write your ass off," Wade offered.

Nods of agreement peppered the table.

"Second, you don't need to find your writer's voice. We all just heard it."

"Well, let me just say again, though, that this is something I would never actually write about," I replied. "I just did this for the exercise."

I had written a very short piece about the death of my father, something that up to that point I had never discussed with anyone, not even my wife, and certainly never put to paper.

"That's fine," Wade responded. "I'm just telling you that based on what you read, you're ready to write a book. Your turn of a phrase is beautiful, the rhythm, the segues, it's all there."

I felt great. But, it did cross my mind: Was he saying this to be kind? Was he saying all of these nice things to make me feel that I got my money's worth? After all, this retreat wasn't free. But what about the others? Their response was just as enthusiastic, and they had nothing to gain by feigning enthusiasm for my writing.

"You know," I began, "I think, more than anything else, I came here for a kick in the ass. I always knew that my biggest problem wouldn't necessarily be finding the words, but sitting down and putting them to paper. Making myself do it. *Believing* I could do it. That's why I came here. And...I just want to thank all of you for what you just gave me. It means more to me than you'll ever know, so thanks."

I am not a crier. I don't usually get weepy but, at that moment I felt the emotions of many years of frustration, mainly with myself, seep to the surface. It was a long time coming.

❦ ❦ ❦

The next day was another writing exercise, which resulted in an even more enthusiastic response. I know I said "Thank you" several times and really tried to impart how much their kind words meant to me, but I'm not sure I managed to express myself that well.

"Matt, you have to write. I'm going to e-mail you and bother you until I see you published," more than one of my fellow writers told me. Basically, those were their parting words: "Write that book!" I didn't realize what they were doing, what they did for me, until several weeks after I returned from the retreat.

They were helping me mark my territory.

❦ ❦ ❦

I left that retreat changed. I wasn't any less insecure or doubtful of my own ability; sadly, I'm pretty sure that will *never* change. Even with all of the kind words, I was still me: quiet, reluctant, not very social, and prone to mood swings. In short, I was my delightful self. But what changed was that I knew, without any doubt, that I would give it my all. I would really try to write a book. I took my dream, the one that has been with me for more years than I care to count, and I peed all over it.

I will never jump out of a plane. Or dive with sharks or

bungee-jump at low altitude. I've got a blank Word document and a blinking cursor. That's scary enough for me, thank you very much. That is my territory. I own it. And I know a Dachshund with a total lack of appreciation for lawn care that would be happy to back me up on that.

Dachshund Life Lesson #8

If it belongs to you, prove it.

CHAPTER 9

Spot Isn't a Name: It's a Location.

There is a moment, fleeting though it may be, when Baxter is putty in my hands. When he forgets to whine to be let out, grumbles for a biscuit, or stares at me until I break like a brittle twig in a strong breeze. It has nothing to do with a test of wills or reverse canine psychology. It's a purely physical thing. An involuntary reflex, for, the sweetest of Baxter's sweet spots, his happiest of happy places, his figurative Achilles' heel, are his ears.

And now, if you have children in the room where you're reading this, you might want to cover *their* ears:

Baxter has eargasms.

"Daddy, do Baxter's spot," my daughter implores.

I take my index and middle fingers and begin to slowly massage just outside Baxter's ear. It doesn't matter which ear; the result is always the same. After a moment or two he slowly pushes his head into the palm of my hand. His eyes immediately go to half-mast. And, his breathing becomes more audible. His body begins to lean as if I'm rubbing the balance right out of him. I think the reason we all get such a kick out of seeing Baxter so at the mercy of my fingers is because, generally speaking, he is never at *our* mercy; we are at *his*. It's more than a little reassuring to know that if push came to shove and I had to find a quick way to subdue him, I've got one. I like to think of it as the Dachshund version of the Vulcan mind meld. And while a rawhide bone or a piece of cheese is Baxter's culinary idea of nirvana, it is my magic fingers that have become Baxter's mental Canyon Ranch and Spa.

It's not uncommon for him to place the side of his head in my hand, giving me the not-so-subtle hint that he's "in the mood." It's actually kind of sweet. It makes me feel like I'm the only person in the world who knows how to immediately, and absolutely, bring him the simplest and purest of joys: feeling good. And I'm always happy to do it. If only all of life's issues could be solved by a little aural stimulation.

I even envy him a little. He knows exactly where his happy place is. Me? I haven't found mine yet. Of course, I'm no longer speaking of a spot on one's body, not that Baxter and I have that kind of relationship. It's just one guy rubbing another guy's ears until that other guy reaches a, uh…never mind.

I'm speaking about geography. A physical location in the world. A place that will not only make me happy, but bring my nomadic search to a blissfully content conclusion. You see, I *am* the wandering Jew.

I've done the math. From about the age of twenty-four, I have moved eighteen times.

No, I have never been in the military, and yes, the fine

folks at U-Haul and I are on a first-name basis. Seems like a lot, right? It seems excessive to me too. But what can I tell you that Bono hasn't already expressed much more melodically: I still haven't found what I'm looking for.

And what would that be?

I wish I knew. I could have saved a fortune on cardboard and packing tape.

So I searched for a place to love. I found plenty of places that I liked for a little while. I found some places whose company I enjoyed for a short time, and then we kind of drifted apart. I had more than a couple of, shall we say, "one-year stands." Hey, I'm not proud of it, but I'm a bit of a relocation slut. A charming cottage in Coral Gables, Florida, didn't do it; a three-story walk-up with parquet floors and a wood-burning fireplace in Albany, New York, didn't speak to me; and a stately colonial in Peachtree City, Georgia, was less a suburban ideal and more like Stepford with a Southern drawl.

Over the years my wife has often called me Pippin. Not because I love lavish, Broadway musical comedy. Okay, not *just* because I love lavish, Broadway musical comedy, but because, like the title character in that show, I was always searching for "my corner of the sky." And, like Pippin, I ultimately realized that what I was searching for wasn't a change in scenery; it was a change in me.

I am writing this sentence as a reluctant resident of New Jersey. I don't really care for New Jersey. If it's the Garden State, then I can see nothing but weeds in my half acre. It is terribly crowded. In fact, New Jersey has the greatest population density of any state. Its real estate taxes are highest in the nation, as well. It *had* a chairman of the board: he's dead. It *had* a Soprano: possibly dead, it wasn't really made clear. And it *has* a Snooki: sadly, she's alive and kicking. Oh, it *does* have a Boss: I'll let that one slide. Two were born here—one was placed here by a writer's vivid imagination, and one of them heard the Jersey Shore was in dire need of high poofs and short drunks. *My* excuse? A job. But while I still work for the same company that I did when I moved here five years ago, I no longer have the same role. I now work from home. So there really is no need for me to live in New Jersey. I can do what I do anywhere. With any luck I will be putting "the Snooki State" in my rearview mirror before too long. Unfortunately, I know from experience that wherever I end up I'll soon find flaws in my new home, cracks in my emotional foundation. I won't be happy. That's okay—truth be told, I don't really *do* "happy."

Basically, I operate in degrees of contentment. There's a chance I will be more content in a different state. I would probably be more content in Minnesota. Or Ohio. Pretty much anywhere. But, in the end it won't really matter because, as I said, "happy" just doesn't seem to be my thing. I'm used to it and so is Melissa. So, don't you worry about me. I'll be content somewhere. It's the *somewhere* that's the hard part.

So, until we can walk into a golden, slightly sulphurous setting sun, with Journey's "Don't Stop Believing" playing in the background, I'll just have to find a way to be hap—oops, somewhat content here in New Jersey. I saw a quote recently that I think sums up my situation rather nicely:

"Bloom where you're planted."

I'm going to need a lot of fertilizer.

Or maybe I should take yet another lesson from Baxter and redefine where "here" is. Maybe it's not about a plot of land or a zip code. Maybe the "here" I need to concern myself with is the real estate between my ears. I mean, it seems to work just great for him.

Now, if only he had opposable thumbs.

Dachshund Life Lesson #9

Be *your happy place.*

CHAPTER 10

OCDog

"Maya, c'mon, let's go inside. C'mon, Maya, inside. Maya! Let's go, c'mon, Maya, time to go inside. *Maya!* Time to go... *Maya!!* It's...*Maya!* C'mooooooon! Jesus Christ, Maya, will you just...*MAYA!!!!!!*"

Since you can't see her right now, let me explain. She is lying on her back, smack-dab in the middle of the driveway, her legs are spread wide open, and she is stock-still and staring at me. This is not a new thing. This is standard operating procedure for Maya. I don't know what kind of life Maya came from before she joined us here at The New Jersey Mental Hospital for Dachshunds, but it really did a number on her. I wish I could say that this was her only, shall we say, curious behavior: It's not.

Take, for instance, the front door. As front doors go, ours is pretty benign. There's no medieval moat to ford, no pointy portcullis to fear, no glaring guards on duty. It's a standard six-panel door painted a dull brown, and with your typical deadbolt lock. It's not a secret portal that leads to some alternate universe where Dachshunds are tortured—not with waterboarding but with water *bathing*. It's just a door we use to enter and exit our home.

But Maya thinks the door is evil.

Maya thinks the door is out to cause her harm.

Maya will not enter the house through the door.

To get Maya to pass through the doorway you have to pick her up and carry her into the foyer.

Baxter and Molly have no door issues. Only Maya. And only with the front door.

She has no problem navigating the garage doors, the sliding patio door, and the interior garage door. She walks, trots, jumps, and runs through those with the carefree agility of a dog free of fear. But the front door absolutely freezes her with terror. I can assure you that while there are many aspects of our home that even *I* find quite terrifying—like our summer electric bill, the stairs that are seemingly being held together with duct tape and prayers, and the shady part of our backyard that local cats have agreed upon as their communal litter box—the front door doesn't even make the cut. Actually, there are extremely rare moments when Maya will, of her own accord and for reasons known only to her, trot right through the front door as if she never, ever had any issues with it. My wife and I will look at each other as if we have seen the hand of God come down from heaven above and perform nothing less than a full-blown miracle.

Until a couple of hours later when the bogey (door)man returns.

The hallway is another of Maya's irrational fears. When

you enter our front door—that is, if you have the balls to enter our front door—you can go one of two ways: up the stairs to the living room or down a short hallway to the kitchen. Maya has lived with us four years and I can't recall—not even once—Maya walking down that hallway. It's probably no more than eight feet in length, with beige walls, white floor molding, and absolutely nothing out of the ordinary about it. Except for the fact that it has never once felt the pitter-patter of Maya's paws upon it.

I've often wondered if perhaps Maya senses something about the hallway that I can't pick up on. Maybe the spirit of a long-dead person who once lived here. If so it would have to be a schmuck of a spirit to spend eternity loitering in a lousy hallway—especially when we have both an enticingly damp basement and a perfectly dusty attic to haunt. A hallway? That's like discovering that a spirit has staked out a claim in your linen closet, or your pantry. Actually, that makes a lot more sense than a hallway; at least a pantry has food, right? The hallway's got nothing going for it.

Stairs. She's not really scared of them; it's more like she questions their motives. Why are they *really* there? Are they meant to help or hinder? Are they designed to afford entry or deny access? Bear in mind we're not exactly talking about the Spanish Steps here. It's four very manageable steps. Four. You couldn't even get a good Slinky run going on these suckers, and here's Maya, pondering their existence as if she were Nietzsche. In a related and equally bizarre note, Baxter has recently started to display his own incomprehensible distrust of stairs. Wonderful! Only in *my* house are phobias commu-nicable.

Another one of Maya's more curious quirks, although at this point we can probably call them what they really are—psychological problems—is that she will never ask to go out-side. When it's time to take out all of the dogs, Maya needs to be carried to the foyer where she will then inexplicably walk through the front door to the grass. And, yes, that's the *same* front door that she will *not* walk through to *enter* the house. Maya would rather lie in her own poop then go outside under her own power. Many dogs will give you some kind of sig-nal that they want to go outside: a bark, an insistent scratch-ing at the door. Maya either has no signal or her signal is so subtle and small that neither the human eye nor ear can detect it. Apparently, I need an electron microscope or Superman's hearing to learn that my dog has to take a dump. About the only hint we receive that Maya needs to answer the call of nature is when we discover a still warm puddle of that nature on the kitchen floor. By that point, it's too little too late.

Maya will rarely jump up on us when we're sitting on the sofa. Whereas Baxter and Molly are all too happy to use our laps as trampolines, Maya will stand on her hind legs, place both of her front paws on the edge of the sofa, and wait patiently for one of us to pick her up and place her on the sofa next to us. A chiropractor recently informed me that I have some bone spurs on my lower back vertebrae, which is my back's way of compensating for excessive stress in that area. Those aren't bone spurs: they're Maya bends. Living with

Maya is like living with a fifteen-pound piece of carpet lint that you're constantly picking up off the floor.

At nine years old she is still fully capable of walking, running, and jumping, which, of course, makes us very happy. There are plenty of dogs with the same background as Maya that aren't nearly as fortunate. Which makes the fact that she usually chooses to not run or jump or walk out the front door even more perplexing. Then again, why wouldn't she? She has *us* to be her legs. It's examples like this that often make me wonder who, exactly, has trained whom.

She is the sweetest, the gentlest, and—with the exception of having us convey her from room to door to grass and back again—the least demanding dog in the world. But she is also a mysterious, often infuriating mass of fears and insecurities brought on, I believe, by a very unhappy past. By providing her with good food, the best medical care, loads of love, and (unfortunately for us) an alternative means of propulsion, we're doing our best to offset that past. In other words, we're Maya's coping mechanism. Nothing unusual there. Then again, she's not the only family member that does weird things in order to deal with the past.

☙ ☙ ☙

I'm neat. I'm organized. I consider spending a couple of hours rehanging clothes and thinning out my closet to be time very well spent. It relaxes me, it allows me to donate clothes to those less fortunate, and it makes the process of deciding what clothes to wear next an easier task. File it under win-win-win!

One day, probably when I was measuring the distance between hangers to ensure that they were all equidistant from each other (I'll leave it to you to mull whether or not I really do that), my wife gave me a look. A combination of a smile and a smirk. The look that says, *Aaaw, your obsessive-compulsiveness is so cute.*

I guess I understood where she was coming from. There is something oddly endearing about watching a loved one do something that while a little out of the ordinary is still sweetly innocent.

"You think I'm nuts, right?" I asked Melissa.

"No, I don't think you're nuts. I think it's just your thing."

"Cleaning is my thing?" I questioned.

"Yeah, it's your downtime, it relaxes you."

"It absolutely relaxes me, but do you know why I really do it?" I asked.

"Because you like your stuff neat and organized," she countered.

"Nope! That's just a by-product of why I really do this."

There is nothing my wife likes more than when I open up about something. I'm not the most emotionally available person, so whenever my wife can tweeze something out of me she's a happy spouse. What was strange about this particular tweezing session was that I, apparently, was doing the plucking.

"So," she uttered with glee, "tell me!"

"My desire to keep things clean, neat, and organized is because of my parents."

This statement prompted a few moments of silence. Mentioning dead parents tends to have that effect on a conversation, especially because it's a subject I don't bring up much.

"Why?" she quietly asked.

I told her.

~ ~ ~

By the time I turned twenty-six both of my parents were dead.

My father from heart disease, my mother from lung cancer, but the real cause in both cases was the same: cigarettes.

They both died very young. I sometimes forget how young until I'm reminded of it. I've often been asked during a first visit with a new physician if I ever had the mumps, measles, and other common childhood illnesses. I usually respond with "I'm not sure." I'm never sure because I don't have a mother to call up and ask.

A doctor recently asked me if diabetes runs in my family. I didn't know. Losing both parents, especially when both they and I were young, leaves more than a massive gap in your life: it leaves lots of spaces on a medical questionnaire hauntingly empty.

My dad died first. Suddenly. Then my mom. Painfully drawn out. Both ways, to put it mildly, sucked. There is nothing I can possibly write about my parents dying that you haven't already read about before in other books about the death of a parent. Unfortunately, at some point, it touches all of us. Nothing I write can possibly shed anything new on the subject. I defer to my previous statement: it *really* sucks! But what makes a parent's death different—or any death, for that matter—is the way you react to it. In that respect, each death is unique, and each of us owns that death in a different way.

Shocked. Numbed. Speechless. Scared. Sad. Overwhelmed. Alone.

I felt them all. Both times. And I was terribly confused. I didn't know what to do, what to say, how to react or *inter*act. I felt like a giant Pause button had been pressed. My mind and emotions were stilled right when something really important was happening: *my life*.

In many ways I guess I was what you would call the classic mourner. I was quiet. I did a lot of staring into space. I didn't know what I was feeling. I was going through the motions. But I never cried.

I might have gotten misty-eyed, but at no point during either of my parents' funerals did I lose it. Not because I was consciously trying *not* to lose it; I just didn't. And there is something about not losing it, not letting it out, that drives those people who do let it out totally crazy. It's as if your mourning isn't official, your loss not real or validated, until you let loose with a torrent of wailing and buckets of tears.

"Hey Matt, you know if you want to cry, it's *okay* to cry."

I wasn't aware I needed formal approval, but thanks for thinking of me.

The truth is, at the time I was sort of wondering myself why I wasn't crying. I was certainly sad enough to warrant tears. Achingly sad. I loved my parents dearly. On paper I seemed like an ideal crying candidate. But, as with many things that look great on paper, the reality was quite different.

Eventually the aluminum trays of half-eaten food were

tossed in the garbage, the metal folding chairs went back in storage, mourners went back to their nonmourning lives, and my brothers and I were left with memories of our parents that were still tacky to the touch.

Memories, especially ones of your parents are supposed to burnish over time to a golden brown, not unlike your parents' skin as they bake under that relentless South Florida sun during their golden years. At that time, my memories of my parents were more like freshly poured cement that needed time to set. To become solid. Time to cure to become an unyielding foundation upon which I could build my own life, my own family. But, until then, my brothers and I were left with two freshly tamped mounds of cold dirt. And the years to think about it.

🦴 🦴 🦴

My closet is divided into three distinct sections: items that hang, items that are shelved, and items that reside on the floor. Within those sections are subsections. Button-down shirts are hung on the top bar in the closet, where they are further divided by color. Polo and T-shirts take up two shelves where, once again, they are divided by colors, as well as by the frequency with which I wear each shirt. And never, ever will a polo shirt be stacked on top of a T-shirt. *Strictly verboten.*

Pants are always hung, never folded, and the zippers of the pants always face the back of the closet. Khakis are placed toward the corner of the closet (I don't wear khakis); jeans reside smack in the middle of the lower bar. Shorts, like the pullover shirts, are divided into two categories: athletic shorts and dress shorts. Dark colors at the bottom of the piles, light colors on top. Shoes reside where you'd expect them to reside: on the floor. I don't have lots of shoes, so they rest comfortably with plenty of distance between each pair, categorized by style and always—*always*—with toes pointing toward the back of the closet. I would gladly explain to you how my chest of drawers is organized, but I think you get the idea.

I often refold laundry because I have a specific way that I like my clothes folded. Most of the items on my desk have a specific spot in which I place them. I will, of my own free will, open the refrigerator and proceed to untangle the mass within, leaving a clean, completely logical, and lovely-to-look-at food *system*.

Some of these things I do because I feel like it and it gives me pleasure. At least, that's what I tell most people. That's even what I tell myself. The truth is that I do these things—refold laundry, line up pens on my desk like planes on a runway, and keep the stack of books on my night table in size order—because I feel that if I don't, bad things could happen.

It sounds crazy to me, too. But that won't prevent me from daydreaming about cleaning out the junk drawer in the kitchen. It certainly won't stop me from doing any of the things I do, because I have a theory that the things that I do are not what they appear to be. I don't recall when I had this revelation about my whole organizing/neatness thing. Odds are it was probably while I was vacuuming. Which, like I say, isn't *really* vacuuming at all. It's remembering.

It's hard to look at two people named Paula and Paul and *not* think that they were meant to be together. People always had the same reaction to that.

"Your names are Paula and Paul? That's so cute."

It was. And, they were.

They were both Brooklyn born and bred, separated by just two years in the shadow of a soon-to-begin World War II. Their world was much different from our own, and I'm convinced that in many ways, it was exceedingly better. A world that could be viewed right from your front stoop; the same stoop that when combined with a ten-cent, rubber Pinky ball, made for some fine afternoon entertainment. It was a time and place where local luncheonettes were landmarks, and a cold egg cream was about the best thing on a hot August day. When I picture it I sort of see the innocent romance of *Happy Days* mixed with the Technicolor grittiness of *West Side Story*. I'm probably not too far off the mark.

They traveled in the same social circles, so I guess it was inevitable that their paths would eventually cross. The names were simply the clincher. They married in 1959.

They had little to speak of. Then again, in 1959, it was amazing what little to speak of could get you. My mom once told me that when her and my dad moved into their first apartment, they had a handful of envelopes, and, on each envelope would be words like *rent*, *electric*, *water*, and *phone*. And every week, when my dad got paid from his job as a short order cook, they would place a certain amount of money in each envelope so by the time the bills came due they would have enough to cover their expenses. My dad was making maybe $40 a week.

Ah, 1959.

I have some scratchy, silent 16 mm movies shot shortly after I was born. My mother waves into the lens, saying words that will never be heard. In her arms is a shock of black hair with a baby's body attached to it, the same black hair that I will see on my daughter's head thirty-eight years later. When you lose parents, especially when they're young, you tend to analyze the little things, the remnants of the life they left behind—because that's all that you have to work with. And whenever I've looked at this old footage, I'm struck by the starkness of the imagery. My mother isn't holding a cell phone. There is no flat panel blaring on the wall behind her. No open laptop on the bed. And the simplicity of that setting makes the attention that my mother is showing me seem, I don't know—real? More meaningful? There's just less to distract, and detract, from the moment. Mom. Me. That's pretty much the composition of the image. I like that image. That's a good remnant.

After a few jerky camera movements, the scene shifts to my aunt Carol and my uncle Jack's house in Oceanside on Long Island. It's my first birthday. There's my wonderful grandmother, my mom's mother, "Nanny." My cousin Mitchell, waving violently into the camera in all of his gawky, preteen glory. There's my cousin Maura, shy and quiet. There's my mom, looking young and happy and every bit the overprotective, coddling Jewish mother. There I am, an already moody, puss-on-his-face toddler. And holding me tightly to his chest is my dad. His body still lean with youth, his hair still black as shoe polish. My aunt Carol just lit the candles on the cake that they probably got from Waldbaum's or A&P. I'm being serenaded with a silent rendition of "Happy Birthday." The camera cuts to a close-up of my dad and me. His cheek is next to mine. He's the only one not singing. He's peppering the tip of my ear with little kisses. A moment later, after some web-like lines crawl across a now shaky camera, the footage burns to white and he is gone.

Remnants.

❧ ❧ ❧

I'm not really organizing my shoes: I'm trying to recall the roughness of my dad's beard when he last hugged me.

I'm not actually cleaning the refrigerator: I'm wishing for an extra five minutes with my mother when she could still recognize who I was.

And I most certainly am not refolding laundry.

Enveloped in that clean, warm scent that always conjures the idea of "home," I am—finally—crying.

❧ ❧ ❧

It's about control.

If I periodically go through my closet and eliminate certain things that either don't fit or I know I will never wear, I am thereby reducing the total amount of items in my closet, which in turn leaves me with less pants to rip, less shirts to stain, less shoes to cause me blisters. Less potential bad things.

If I organize my desk, I know exactly where to find everything that I need. Nothing ever goes missing because I will not allow it. I don't waste time searching for that certain black marker that I like, because that certain black marker that I like is where I left it. Always. Something that is not where it's supposed to be is a bad thing. I eliminate bad things.

On a horrible day in March 1981, a doctor looked me square in the eye and told me that my dad was going to die; a week later he was proven right.

There was an awful, awful moment in February 1988, when my mother looked at me and called me by a name other than the one she gave me. She passed away early the next morning.

I do what I do because somewhere in my still-saddened, residually wrecked mind, I am trying to gain control over that which I *can* control: clothing and cleaning, organizing and allocating. Trivial things. Minor gestures born from a major loss. I do what I do because on two absolutely horrific days, I controlled absolutely nothing.

But I'm not a stupid person. I consider myself fairly logical, so I know that it all means nothing. All of the cleaning and organizing and eliminating I do will have no impact on keeping the bad things and bad moments in life at bay. They're coming, I get it, I truly do. But trying to convince me of that will yield little results for, you see, you wouldn't be reasoning with *me*. You'd be talking to a nineteen-year-old boy and having a heart-to-heart with a twenty-six-year-old young man who both want but will never get the same exact thing: they want their mom and dad back.

Me? I'm just refolding, scouring, and vacuuming. Where's the harm in that?

Bone divider

"So *that's* the reason," Melissa says. "Given what you went through with your parents, I can see how that makes sense."

"I don't know if I would say it makes *sense*. It just is what it is."

"Whatever it *is*, I love you. Now, go mop the floor," she jokes.

And that was where my wife and I netted out in regards to my control issue. Although it really is a reminder of the lengths a subconscious will go to just to not rock the boat. Or, at least, provide us with some emotional Dramamine.

Left to their own devices, our minds can be quite the little mad scientists, testing and teasing one minute, soothing and satisfying the next. And that makes for some memories that manifest themselves in some very strange ways. I'm proof of that.

And so is Maya. Which is why I try to cut her as much slack as I can. I like to think she would do the same for me.

For all I know, all of the little tics and quirks and habits that often lead to her moaning—and me cursing a blue streak—is simply her best attempt to deal with her past. Maybe her fear of entering through the front door and her hallway phobia and her suspicion of stairs is just her past being present. But why she leaves her partially chewed rawhide chips willy-nilly all over the house is beyond me. It drives me nuts.

But, whatever: I can control only so much.

Dachshund Life Lesson #10

Even with a messy past, the present can still be pretty neat.

CHAPTER **11**

Dog in a Blanket

I love my bed.

Like, *love*!

California king. Sealy Posturepedic. Sure Rest. Memory foam topper. Three-hundred-count Egyptian cotton sheets. Goose down comforter, filled by some of the most selfless geese I've ever had the pleasure of sleeping on. And my bed is positioned in such a way that it catches the first crisp chill of autumn and the warm, lazy breezes of summer, creating an expansive, seductive envelope of sleep-inducing comfort. And yet, I don't really care about my bed.

I lie on it, roll in it, drool upon it, toss and turn within its inviting folds and delicious divots. I luxuriously wallow in its depths like a depressed boar pig, in my all-too-frequent attempts to keep the world at bay. But every morning I leave my bed. Unmade, untended—and ultimately unloved.

Unlike Molly's blanket.

🦴 🦴 🦴

Molly and her blanket were a package deal.

When we first picked Molly up at Newark Airport she

came wrapped in this sweet, little plaid blanket. There she was, peering out from behind the grill of the carrier, all wrapped up in her soft little shroud, a shorthaired, piebald beggar looking for a handout: *Spare some kibble?*

Like all blankets, Molly's has been used primarily for warmth. Molly is pretty small and it doesn't take much more than a strong sneeze in her direction to get her shivering. But Molly's blanket serves double duty: it serves doggie doody.

Yes, it's not uncommon to detect the telltale funk of poop and trace its origin to Molly's blanket, an unfortunate victim of a lazy bowel movement or what my wife and I have come to refer to as danglers. Vomit? That's a given, given the fact that Molly ingests certain items that have no business being ingested by a dog who has obvious trouble discerning what is and isn't edible. There's also the residue that occurs when Molly is gnawing on one of her rawhide chips. But the word *residue* never really captured the nastiness of this slimy yet somehow still-gritty by-product of her enjoyment. We call it smock, which, ironically, is what one should be wearing if you're going to attempt to manipulate one of these things. Try plucking an eel from a tank of petroleum jelly and you'll begin to understand. But as slippery as these things are, I'm pretty sure that one of the ingredients in these bones is glue, because if we don't wipe off the smock right after Molly is done applying it to the sofa, it's there for good. I have yet to meet a stain protectant that can protect our furniture from smock. But, I was talking about Molly's blanket. It's pretty much a wreck. It has gone from a jolly tartan plaid, reminiscent of the Scottish highlands, to a caked-on, muted mélange of what was once a jaunty spectrum of color.

It has been faded by hundreds of washings and harsh detergents. It is tattered and torn to the point where referring to it *as* a blanket is an insult to fine, upstanding blankets the world over. Every day it resides on the very precipice of taking that long and final fall into the garbage can. But then I see Molly with her blanket, and it lives to see another day.

Baxter and Maya also have their special items. For Baxter it's a giant pink beanbag. And like many of the things that Baxter now claims as his, the beanbag was previously owned by a human. We had bought it for Emmy. She wanted a huge one. So we bought her a beanbag we thought would be huge. It wasn't. It was bigger than huge. Lifting this thing is a two-person job. Eventually, we had to take it out of Emmy's room because it was no longer Emmy's room: it was the beanbag's room. We temporarily placed it in a corner of the family room until we could think of somewhere else to put it. However, at some point during this time, a four-legged member of the family found the Jupiter-sized beanbag much to his liking. At that point, Emmy's beanbag became Baxter's beanbag. It hasn't moved. For all I know, it's taken root. But there, right in the middle of its neon pinkness, is a Baxter-sized indentation. And I see neither the giant beanbag nor its current occupant moving anytime soon.

And then there's Maya's pillow. It's one of the two pillows that came with the new sectional sofa we purchased not too long ago. We bought the sofa because we loved the color, the material, the size, and the price, and it was really comfortable.

At least to us humans. Maya's opinion differed. Not too long after we got the sofa Maya decided the seat cushions needed a bit more cushioning. She slowly stepped onto one of the throw pillows, curled her body nose to tail, and she hasn't budged since. When Maya comes onto the couch it is a two-step process. The first step is someone picking up Maya and placing her on the couch, and then taking her pillow and placing it exactly at the deepest corner of the sectional. In fact, when Maya is placed on the sofa, and her pillow isn't placed where it should be, she will simply stand there and look at Melissa or myself, until one of us takes the hint and rights this terrible wrong. Like most things with Dachshunds, it's partly sweet and partly annoying. But, no matter how much Maya loves her pillow or Baxter adores his giant beanbag, neither compare to the love Molly has for her blanket.

Have you ever witnessed anyone practicing the ancient Japanese art of Origami? The gentle precision of the cuts, the careful pressure applied to each and every calculated fold, and the exacting patience given to creating something that is as fragile as it is breathtakingly beautiful? That begins to approach how Molly feels about her blanket.

With her little, totally inadequate paws, she molds and sculpts her blanket into a shape and design known only to her. A bit of a crimp here, some more height where it leans against the pillow of the sofa, maybe a smidge of compression where pillow meets seat cushion. She will spend two minutes doing this; she will spend *ten* minutes doing this. And, when she's doing this right next to you it can be surprisingly irritating, if it weren't for the fact that it's also hypnotically fascinating.

Cats are supposed to be finicky, not Dachshunds. But, she moves about, nipping and tucking, fluffing and folding, arranging her blanket for optimal comfort while at the same time treating it like it's a new objet d'art that she's decided the room was in desperate need of. She's Nate Berkus with dewclaws. And, can I tell you something? She does fabulous work.

Once satisfied with her work, she starts to methodically walk on the blanket, round and round she goes, when will she stop, who the hell knows? But, eventually she does stop, finally settling in to what has become a uniquely shaped, perfectly coiffed, Molly-sized nest of warmth, security, and comfort.

I wish I felt that way about something.

Something that was so precious to me, so profoundly important, that I would be willing to spend any amount of time tending to its care. Gladly run the risk of being considered a fool for doing whatever necessary to ensure its place of honor in my life.

Obviously I feel that way about my wife and daughter—that's a given. I'm talking about something else. A material object that, while benign and seemingly meaningless to everyone else, means so much to me that I couldn't even sufficiently express *why* to someone else. And, even if I did, it wouldn't make any sense to them. Wait! I've got it! I do have something—and, like Molly's blanket, it's a connection to my past. An always-there, comforting touchstone. And, just like Molly's blanket, ugly as sin.

I have this sweater...

I remember mah-jongg.

I recall canasta.

And I have a faint recollection of something to do with cutting out pictures from magazines, gluing them to a metal lunch box, and coating them with shellac. Decoupage, I believe they called it. I could be wrong—there were a lot of fumes wafting through the air in those days.

All I know for sure is that my mom was always playing something or making something. Whether it involved a folding card table, a wedge of brie, and an ungodly amount of onion dip, or fabric shears, silk flowers, and Elmer's Glue, my mom was game. Neither she nor her girlfriends seemed to actually excel at whatever they were doing at any particular time, but I don't think they set a high achievement bar to begin with. I think they viewed their little sessions as nothing more than a reason to laugh and gossip, bitch and moan, and contribute to the Ernest and Julio Gallo fund. The ladies of the Beach Haven development in Brooklyn were nothing if not philanthropic. And, generally speaking, blitzed.

But right after the mah-jongg and before the canasta, I remember a knitting phase.

I vividly recall a large straw bag, the kind you would get on a trip to the Bahamas, which was pretty impressive when you consider the fact that my parents never went to the Bahamas. I have no idea how that bag got to our apartment. The only vacations I remember were long, sweat-filled drives to the Amish country, where the only straw I remember seeing was filled with manure. But this bag was just bursting with brightly colored rolls of wool—*skeins*, in the proper knitting vernacular. Tons of the stuff. A veritable rainbow of wondrous, wooly, itchy possibilities. Apparently, Mom had big plans. And I most definitely remember seeing these pink, foot-long knitting needles slashing the air as my mom manipulated them in an effort to craft a...something. I don't actually know what she was shooting for, but her fingers were whaling on that wool like nobody's business.

At some point in her knitting period she got it into her head that she was going to knit my dad a sweater. Not content to stay in the shallow end of the knitting pool, Mom was preparing to do a big, old, ugly belly flop, complete with a rolled neck and cuffed sleeves. I don't know how long it took her. To be honest with you, I was busy growing up and focusing on things like convincing my parents that to be a happy, well-adjusted nine-year-old, I desperately needed a new Schwinn bike with a sparkly red banana seat and a sissy bar. You know, important stuff. But one day I saw it.

I slowly pulled it out, holding it away from my body, like a scratchy, poisonous snake. It just kept coming and coming. I looked it up and down. And I have to tell you, my mom really pulled it off. She made the ugliest sweater it has ever been my misfortune to behold. It boasted this misaligned blue-and-white zigzag pattern, and the neck part wasn't a rolled collar as I had heard during all my mother's pre-sweater buzz; it was like some grotesque demon spawn of a mock turtleneck collar and a real turtleneck collar: a murtle collar. And the sleeves? Okay, by some fluke she had managed to make the sleeves the same length. But the shoulders: one looked like it was meant to cover a football player's shoulder pad and the other that same football player's penis. This wasn't just a poorly crafted sweater, it was a genuinely disturbing piece of knitwear.

"Mom, did Daddy see that?" I inquired shortly after seeing this monstrosity.

"No, not yet."

"So, you're going to show it to him?"

"Of course. Why wouldn't I?"

Apparently, whatever chemicals are used in the wool dyeing process were released while my mother was knitting, thereby leaving her with a deeply flawed sense of reality, to say nothing of fashion sense.

"Ma, it doesn't really look…right," I said gently.

She took it from my hands and held it up in front of herself, as if she was considering wearing it.

"Sure, the measurements are a little off, but Daddy will love it, trust me."

A little off, not unlike Mom's deeply skewed judgment.

All I could muster was "Okay."

I probably left the room under the guise of having to attend a pressing game of stickball that I just could not get out of, or something. The truth is that my mom, and that freaking Frankensweater, were both starting to creep me out.

🦴 🦴 🦴

He loved it.

Seriously, he *loved* that deeply flawed excuse of a sweater.

Of course, he didn't wear it—he *couldn't* wear it. But he made such a to-do over that thing you would have thought that he had just been given the finest cashmere cardigan that money could buy. At that point the sweater took its rightful place somewhere deep in the dark bowels of my dad's closet.

"Do I know your father or do I know you father?" my mom posed to me in triumph.

"Yep, you sure do."

She was my mother. What was I supposed to say?

🦴 🦴 🦴

If you were to open the door to my closet and look up toward the top shelf, you would see a pretty random-looking pile of clothes. In it are a couple of paint-splattered polo shirts that I use when a couple coats of Sherwin Williams's best is called for. There is a terribly worn, flaccid-looking pair of sweatpants that my wife will have to pry from under my cold, dead ass before I'd peel 'em off and let her trash them. There's a red-and-gray flannel shirt that I can't, for the life of me, ever recall buying, but the thing's been there so long I feel bad getting rid of it. *Maybe one day,* I tell myself. That day ain't today, and it probably won't be tomorrow. And then at the very bottom of this pile of garbage clothes is the most god-awful sweater you've ever seen. I don't know how it came to be in my possession. I never asked for it, it was never offered to me, and yet there it is. It has been with me for years.

I have thought many times about getting rid of it.

I can't.

Wearing it certainly isn't an option.

It has no earthly purpose or practical reason to continue to reside on that tippy-top shelf in my closet except for one: it fills my heart.

It reminds me of a life long before the words *tumor* and *cancer* changed that life forever. Long before I knew just how important memories really are. It's a hideous, beautiful, ill-shaped, perfectly formed, goes-with-nothing, goes-with-everything memory of what was.

And so, just like Molly, I tend to my sweater.

Whenever I'm weeding out my closet I'll always take it down from its perch and refold it, fluff it, and always make sure that it sits squarely on the shelf, never to endure a nasty fall. But mostly, I tend to my sweater so I don't forget it's there.

🦴 🦴 🦴

As I stare at Molly sheltered within the woolen walls of her sad blanket, I no longer question her behavior or motives. It makes absolute sense. Molly has taught me that true value, true meaning, has nothing to do with appearance, condition, or status. It's all about how that certain something makes you feel, and sometimes what it makes you remember. There she goes again, pushing and shoving and positioning her blanket so it's exactly the way she wants it. I wonder if she'd mind making some room for me.

Dachshund Life Lesson #11

Beauty (including blankets and sweaters) is in the eye of the beholder.

CHAPTER 12

Let 'Er Rip!

If Baxter's bladder can be summarily categorized as nervous, his ass is supremely confident. No! Confident isn't even a strong enough word. *Brash!* That's it: Baxter has a brash ass.

With poop he is prodigious; with farting he is nothing short of phenomenal. Now, for those of you out there who think that all this fart talk is more than a bit infantile, I'll have you know that there once was a time—and what a glorious time it was—when farting was a bona fide form of entertainment. I shit you not!

Look, now's as good a time as any to tell you that there's going to be a fair amount of this cheap wordplay like that "shit you not" line going on for the next few pages, so if you're not into that kind of thing, if you're above potty humor, I suggest flipping ahead to the next chapter. Seriously, I won't be offended in any way. I'll see you in a bit.

🦴 🦴 🦴

Stinking around huh? Ooops! I mean *sticking* around. Hey, you can't say you weren't warned. Where was I?

Joseph Pujol was a Frenchman who was famous for his

remarkable ability to fart at will. The profession, yes, it was an actual job, was referred to as "flatulist," "farteur," or my personal favorite, "fartiste." Picasso had a blue period; Joseph Pujol just had gas.

Well, apparently, in homage to those who came before him, Baxter, unlike Justin Timberlake, is opting to bring something *else* back, and in a really big way.

🦴 🦴 🦴

As a society we frown upon farting. Who am I kidding? We do *way* more than frown upon it: we mock it, we ridicule it, we accuse others of doing it. *Frown?* I frown if I have to wait more than ten minutes for a table. I frown if I get behind the wrong line of cars at the toll plaza. *Purposeful, public displays of farting?* I'm afraid, my friend, that at that point, we've entered into the no-turning-back realm of shunning. And yet, there is something about the act of farting that we all, yes, even you, find amusing in some strange way. Think I'm wrong? Then why is it when someone farts the reaction almost always includes a certain degree of laughter? Those tears rolling down your face aren't tears of disgust. Okay, they're not *just* tears of disgust, they're also tears of silliness. They're memories of farting contests at age nine with the same group of friends that you'll no doubt see again at thirteen, when you'll discover the joys of other bodily functions. Memories of submission by fart when you sat on your brother's head and shouted, "Release the hounds," and then proceeded to do so. For crying out loud, a hundred years ago some French guy paid for his café au laits and croissants with farts! Don't tell me we don't hold a teeny, tiny place in our hearts for our old friend the fart. One look at all of the ridiculous names we've developed for it is proof enough of that:

Ripping one
Cracking a rat
Stepping on a duck
Gassing
Crapdusting
Odorizing
Tearing one off
Air raid
Anal air
Fecal fumigation
Awful aerosol
Dousing
Pooper spray

Trust me: if you go through the trouble of giving something more nicknames than a once-treasured teddy bear that you slept with until sophomore year, there's something about it you like. Okay, not like. Find funny—how's that? It's like when little boys used to pull the pigtails of the little girls that sat in front of them in second grade. You said you didn't like her, but we all knew the truth. We also know this truth: nobody ever wants to take the blame for "detonating an instinkiary device."

(I can go all day, folks.)

Of course not! Who in their right mind wants to own up to

the fact that you just, even accidentally, committed the most offensive, reprehensible societal faux pas possible? We won't even cop to it in our own homes!

What are you looking at me for? It was the dog! should ring a bell to all of us.

And in some instances and in some houses that bell rings true, terrible, and—seemingly—every hour on the hour.

In my house it's practically money in the bank.

　　　🦴 🦴 🦴

In the parlance of farting, Baxter is what's called a habitual. In other words, he is almost always the guilty farty. (Someone should really be writing these down—other than me, I mean.) How much does he fart? Let's just say it's enough that you desperately wished he wouldn't. And, it's not like we feed him anything out of the norm to contribute to his butt burps (I literally just made that one up—didn't even take me that long). And as far as we know, he has no physiological issue that would contribute to his tooting tendency (like shooting fish in a barrel). And he's certainly not doing it for shits and giggles; he already does enough of the first and is incapable of the latter. Baxter farts for that most obvious and logical of reasons: he's a dog, and dogs fart. But unlike humans, dogs don't seem to give a crap about farting. Why should they? To them it's simply another scent in the olfactory rainbow that is a dog's world.

Baxter barely acknowledges when he lets one launch. On rare occasions, when he's lounging on the couch and casually rips a nasty, he will ever so slightly raise his head, point his nose toward his backside, and gently sniff. He'll then glance at me with an accusatory eye and return his head to the pillow. Ah, life is good. And by *good* I mean nose-hair-curling foul.

This is going to sound strange. Granted, you're reading a chapter focused squarely on the subject of farting, so I suppose "strange" is relative, but, I kinda wish I was more like Baxter. Not the fact that we're constantly bombarded with an aerial assault of foulness I wouldn't subject upon my worst enemy. I'm talking about his total lack of caring or concern when he farts. I know we've already established that Baxter doesn't have a clue what the hell's going on back there, but he's just so blasé about it, so utterly devoid of expression, that I can't help but imagine that what I'm witnessing is a classic—maybe even *the* classic example—of not giving a shit.

"Baxter! What are you doing? You're killing Daddy."

Nary a ripple of concern crosses his face while oodles of noxious, invisible ripples are being launched from his rear. I was recently lying on the couch one lazy Sunday afternoon watching a football game when I caught a whiff of Baxter's latest and not-so-greatest creation. I glanced to my side and there he was, an immobile, beached, black-and-tan blob with a sphincter that just wouldn't shut the hell up. Unconcerned. Unabashed. Un-*everything*.

The teams went to the locker rooms with the score tied.

I went to the mirror with a nagging question.

🦴 🦴 🦴

I have always been worried about what people think of me. Concerned about their opinions of what I do, what I say, what

I think. And I don't know why. As far as I can recall, I never experienced some traumatic event that would be the reason behind this fact. What I can tell you is that I wish I wasn't a worrier. I'm thoroughly convinced that people who don't care about what others think of them live more blissful, happier, carefree lives than those who do. Me? I'm worried if I'm *not* worrying about something.

"I swear, you're not happy unless you're miserable," I've often been told.

And, after years of denying and fighting that statement I've finally come to accept it for what it is: the unfortunate truth.

I am a constantly concerned, always-dreading, glass-is-half-empty, waiting-for-the-other-shoe-to-drop, card-carrying member of the worriers club. I wish I had a dollar for every time someone has posed the following question to me:

"Why can't you just stop worrying and be happy?"

Let me once and for all make something crystal clear to all of my concerned fans. I *can* be happy. I've *been* happy many, many times in my life, for reasons both large and small. Here's the distinction: I seem to let people and their opinions get in the way of me being happy. So, to review: I *can* be happy, but I have trouble *letting* myself be happy, primarily due to the outside influences of, well, people. Ergo, I worry. We good on that?

My parents were great. I know they loved me, took care of me, clothed me, fed me, sent me to school, and in general did all of the things in the Parenting 101 handbook. My brothers and I never wanted for anything. We were raised in an average lower-middle-class home where, at least in hindsight, nothing traumatic ever happened. I bring this up because I think I was given the love and attention that should more or less yield a well-adjusted person with a solid sense of self-esteem, and not the morose, negative, always-assuming-the-worst person that I've seem to become. So if it wasn't them it has to be me, right?

Let me just check something. Sit tight.

Born in March of '62, Pisces, emotional, lives in a dream world, loyal, creative, avoids confrontation, puts far too much credence in horoscopes, oldest of three sons, carried mantle of overachieving first child smack into the middle of the 50th percentile, coped with crushing case of shyness during early teens, took public speaking class, became less shy, joined football team, joined baseball team, joined drama club thereby negating any cool quotient gained from joining the aforementioned football and baseball teams, late bloomer with girls, first high school girlfriend was last high school girlfriend, family moved to California after graduation, broke up with girlfriend, devastated, personal torment, etc., father dies, moves back to New York, pines for high school girlfriend, endures a regrettable wardrobe phase that featured purple surgical pants and white Capezio dance shoes, permed his hair, met a new girl, fell deeply in love made all the more remarkable considering previously mentioned wardrobe and hairstyle choices, dated girl, loved girl, had sex for the first time at nineteen with girl, convinced he was going to marry the girl, breaks up with girl, loses weight, loses will to live, drown sorrows in several thousand 7&7s and Alabama Slammers (quite popular in the '80s), finds first crappy job, finds second crappy job, commutes into Manhattan, meets new girl, transitions from second crappy job to new awesome job...that quickly turns crappy, meets best friend of then-current girlfriend, falls in love with best friend, awkwardness ensues, gets engaged to best friend, mother dies, gets married, moves to upstate New York only to find snow and...more crappy jobs, moves to Florida, rents apartment, can't even find a crappy job, tension, arguments, roving eyes, pain, sadness, divorce, a couple years of serial dating, finds good job, becomes better job, meets woman, falls in love, gets married, has beautiful daughter, moves to Georgia, adopts Dachshund, immediately regrets decision to adopt Dachshund, moves to New Jersey, currently regretting decision to move to New Jersey, adopts two more Dachshunds, job going well, Dachshund count holding steady at three, currently finishing writing this sentence.

I don't get it.

Some ups, some downs, but certainly not an overwhelming avalanche of sadness and despair, more like periodic showers of unfortunate events and circumstances. So, I don't really understand why I can't just be who I am without worrying about every little thing. Why do opinions matter to me so much? Why do I need validation? Why can't what *I* think of me be the only opinion that matters? That question dogged me for a very long time, right up to the moment when those two football teams went into the locker room, because it was at that moment when Baxter blasted me with a dose of reality and realization.

He's a dog.

That was it.

He doesn't care about farting, because in order to care you must be aware of yourself and conscious of what you do, and dogs aren't built that way. If you're looking to learn how to best contort your body in such a way that enables you to provide your genital region with a slow, deliberate tongue bath, I thoroughly and quite willingly defer to the canine in the corner that's currently attending a party between his hind legs. But if you're looking for a banner example of self-awareness, dogs ain't it. That's just the way they are: wonderfully oblivious.

🦴 🦴 🦴

I worry, and there is nothing wrong with that. I worry because I want to keep myself and my family safe. I worry because the opinion of certain people, like it or not, holds certain value for me. I worry because I want my daughter to live in a world where parents don't have to worry—which, of course, will never happen. I guess that's the one thing that worriers need not ever worry about: running *out* of things to worry about.

Look, I'm not perfect. I don't have all the answers, I often fall short of my goals, I don't always say or do the right thing and I sometimes hurt people when I don't mean to.

On the other hand, I obey all laws, pay my taxes, try to be polite, always give that little wave of acknowledgment whenever someone lets me into traffic. I work hard, I'm a good neighbor, I don't litter, I leave good tips in restaurants, and I do a bunch of other stuff that makes me realize that, all in all, I'm a pretty decent person. And that being a decent person, in a world that often looks like it's lost any shred of decency, is not a bad thing to be.

Nobody's keeping score on me. Nobody's really paying attention to what I say and do, mainly because they're too busy paying attention to themselves, and I suppose there's a lesson in that. I need to focus on what *I* think of me. Not to go all Stuart Smalley on you, but I think I'm good enough—not as good as some—but certainly better than many. While I might not be ready for the *Jeopardy!* Tournament of Champions, I don't think I would embarrass myself during the Teen Tournament, which can certainly be grueling—I mean, some of those questions are pretty hard. Seriously. They're not gimmes. And, as I approach the age of fifty I think that for the most part, most people have liked me; fortunately, some have even loved me.

I think that fifty thing has something to do with all of this. I think you reach a certain age and you realize that you're coming to a point where maybe you should take stock of your life. Start checking off boxes. I've spent the first forty-nine years going up that first big hill on a roller coaster, and fifty is like being at the top of that hill the moment right before your ass begins to rise from the seat and your stomach begins to rise in your throat. And the rest is one long (albeit not nearly as long as you thought it would be), exciting, scary, wonderful, stressful, exhilarating, emotional, meaningful, memorable ride.

I'm good with fifty. *I'm great with fifty!*

Neither of my parents even got close to fifty, so I feel very lucky. I have a wife who loves me and whom I love dearly, and a daughter who fills my heart to nearly bursting every day. I have a good job where people respect me. I have a roof over my head and food in my belly.

So I guess after some of the boxes have been ticked off and the forty-nine years have been lived, it's fair to say that there have been challenges and disappointments and deaths and separations and bad choices and bad jobs and days when I seriously wondered if there wasn't some grand, cosmic conspiracy against me. It took me forty-nine years to realize what it really was: life. Nothing more. Nothing less. But the good has far outweighed the bad, and I really hope that trend continues. I've certainly learned my fair share of life lessons, most recently from the hindquarters of a Dachshund—namely, that there are worse things in life than being a worrier.

So, that's the end of all the silly fart talk and definitely the end of worrying about worrying. Seriously, because it just stinks.

Okay, that *really* is the end. And with apologies to Bobby McFerrin...

Dachshund Life Lesson #12

Don't worry—be gassy.

CHAPTER 13

Slow Down, Where's the Fire Hydrant?

Maya might be a Buddhist.

Or lazy.

Or both.

Hard to say.

Because, I can't tell if she's calmly meditating, trying to harness her chi or whatever it is that Buddhists enjoy harnessing, or she's come to the somewhat radical decision to not move at all and simply let the world come to her. She neither shaves her head, burns incense, nor has she shown any inclination to follow Richard Gere on Twitter, so I'm leaning toward the lazy thing.

Long story short: Maya doesn't move much.

🦴 🦴 🦴

When Maya receives a treat it is exactly that. She will sit on the sofa or wait at the top of the stairs and *receive* her treat. She never meets her treat halfway. Maya will bark like crazy when someone rings the bell or a strange car pulls into the driveway, but she will never go down the stairs and approach the front door like Baxter and Molly do. Maya has to be royally conveyed to her food bowl. Maya would prefer to be stepped on by one of the other dogs as opposed to moving an inch that would help her avoid being stepped on. Melissa or I usually intervene and move her out of harm's way. Watch Maya for a short while, and it quickly becomes obvious that Maya finds moving highly overrated. Strike that—Maya finds moving *fast* overrated. If the Greyhound is the cheetah of the dog world, then Maya is the tortoise. Which is really strange, because when she wants to, Maya can run pretty fast. I've seen it on a handful of occasions: her legs pumping, her head bobbing, tongue lolling out of the side of her mouth. She's totally capable, but it would seem that she chooses not to.

"Maya! Get the squirrel! Go ahead, Maya! Squirrel! Maya, go get it! *Go get it!!*"

Not interested.

"Hang on Maya, let me get you a cup of Darjeeling and a copy of the *New Yorker* instead."

Squirrels? Birds? Cats? Deer? Same response: Maya staring at me amazed at *my* fascination with small woodland creatures. About the only time Maya will intentionally move fast is during winter, when she has to go to the bathroom and wants to limit the amount of time she has to spend sticking her butt into a stiff north wind.

Recently there was a deer in our yard, and I don't mean a vague, dusky form that you can sort of make out through two hundred yards of closely quartered oaks and firs. This deer was standing in plain sight on our patio. Most deer that roam through our yard take off at the slightest hint of our presence. This thing was standing there wondering when I was going to start throwing some burgers and dogs on the grill. Maya would never get another chance like this. I could practically see her nipping at the deer's hooves, could practically see Maya and the deer act out a scenario that had been going on for thousands of years: The female lion crouches in the tall grass, intently eyeing her prey, her stare unwavering. An antelope chews on an acacia bush, completely unaware. Then, in a burst of tawny fur and primal power, the lion launches itself into the air and lands on the back of the antelope, slamming its jaws together into the antelope's neck and quickly bringing to an end another brutal, yet somehow beautiful life-and-death struggle.

Apparently, Maya, like the deer, was waiting for the burgers.

She didn't show even the slightest desire to chase the deer. At that moment it was hard to believe that Maya was descended from wolves. It would have taken less of a leap of faith to believe she was descended from sloths. There I was, jumping up and down like a lunatic, practically screaming at her to get the deer!

Not a budge.

After we went back into the house, I sat down on the sofa and glanced over at Maya, who had already settled back into the big, brown chair and her routine of, well, settling back into the big, brown chair. She let out a deep sigh and slowly closed her eyes. Shortly after that I heard the slow, reassuring rhythm of her preslumber breathing. Right before she dozed off, she opened one of her eyes and gave me a look as if to ask, *What did all that effort and running around get you?*

I took some time to think about that.

❦ ❦ ❦

I'm an early arriver. Always.

It doesn't matter where I'm going—it could be to a doctor's appointment or simply to get a haircut—I always show up before I'm supposed to. The thought of having to run through an airport because I didn't leave enough time to get there, park the car, and go through security is what keeps me leaving for the airport long before my flight is due to depart.

This past summer we drove to Virginia on vacation. In order to bypass the notoriously bad traffic that surrounds our nation's capital, I suggested we leave before dawn. Melissa suggested separate vacations.

We left around nine-ish.

It's a constant battle, my having to always beat the clock and, consequently, anyone else who is also looking to beat time into submission. I must say, though, I'm not as bad as I used to be. And I know exactly when I became less obsessed with rushing. Ironically, it was when time itself seemed to be taking its own sweet-ass time.

❦ ❦ ❦

It is perhaps the world's worst-kept secret that men have little, bordering on nothing, to do with the birthing process. Other than sitting in a chair, staring at my wife and telepathically willing her cervix to dilate to 10, my role on November 1, 2000, was not what you would call mission critical. In a nutshell: I waited.

My wife had gone through this before with the birth of my stepson, so she had a point of reference from which to pull from, a glossary of what to expect. This was my first child. And even though I read all of the books that a new dad is supposed to read and asked lots of questions, when the actual day arrived I did what I always tend to do when I get very stressed: I shut up and stared. It's important to go with your strengths.

"Are you okay?" asked my wife, who was preparing to expel another person from her body.

"Yep, I'm good," I remember responding, with about as much emotion and enthusiasm as a man who was about to watch his wife's vagina become an exit point could muster.

We arrived at the hospital around 11:00 that morning, and it was probably around 2:00 when it was time for the epidural. I remember watching Melissa's eyes glaze over when the doctor uttered that singularly magical word. When the anesthesiologist came in to administer the epidural, I recall him doing this whole spiel about how, because it's a procedure that involves the spine, there's always a remote chance of paralysis should something go terribly wrong. I don't think Melissa had much concern at that point based on her response of "Yep, got it, paralysis, just do it, it's fine, just do it." He did it.

I don't know if I have ever seen my wife look as angelically happy as she did when that epidural kicked in.

"So, feeling better, babe?" I stupidly asked, when I could

have just looked at the wave of sheer joy that washed across my wife's face and stopped washing about an inch above her belly button. If epidurals were available for public consumption, and if they were considered a viable option for, say, gift giving around the holidays, I'd be cued up year in and year out for a few miraculous cc's worth. Epidural: the gift that keeps on taking away.

And so we sat like that: me, utterly mute in my recliner in the distant corner; my wife in her bed, beaming from the sensation of no longer feeling any sensation. Well, my telepathic suggestions must have been on delay or something, because a couple of hours later her cervix finally got the message.

"Looks good, were at 10," the doctor proclaimed. "Time to start pushing."

My stomach dropped.

Oh shit, pushing!

Something about the word *pushing* at that particular moment just didn't sound right. With an experience that, by all accounts, was "beautiful," "peaceful," and "godly," about to happen, "pushing" seemed, I don't know, just about the most wrong action to undertake. If you're moving a sofa and it gets stuck in a doorway, "pushing" is your man. If someone angrily gets in your face, "pushing" is probably your go-to move. But when your wife is about to bring forth the precious life that has been quietly, perfectly gestating in her womb for the past nine months, "pushing" becomes one helluva buzzkill.

So this is actually going to happen, I thought to myself.

For some reason I sort of forgot that there was an objective for this whole thing, that it wasn't just about sitting around

146

and staring—but I'll be honest with you: I kinda hoped it was, because I was nailing it!

🦴 🦴 🦴

They moved the bed under an array of lights that in a former life illuminated some minor-league ballpark. I slowly, and probably a little reluctantly, walked over to the side of the bed where I witnessed the nurses hiking up my wife's dressing gown—way up—and then placing her feet into the stirrups, which quickly reminded me that this most definitely was *my* first rodeo. The harsh glare of those lights on all of those shiny, cold, sterilized metal instruments made me wonder if maybe Edward Scissorhands, coming off of a very bad break-up with Winona Ryder, decided to go into obstetrics. I was indeed relieved to see that our doctor had ten fingers and that none required any kind of sharpening maintenance.

Melissa started to push. *God*, did she push! She started to make sounds. I never realized just how long a minute actually was until it was filled with the kind of full-throated, no-holds-barred yelling that occurs when someone is trying to expel a bowling ball through a space that was in no way built to allow a bowling ball to pass through it. Except, by some miracle, it does.

The doctor encouraged me to take a look.

I leaned down toward where all the action seemed to be happening. And it was there that I saw the top of a small, wet human head beginning to emerge from inside my wife.

I have seen the sun come up over the Smoky Mountains, I have seen a glacier calving in the Inside Passage of Alaska, and I have seen the *Mona Lisa*. (Okay, maybe I just caught a glimpse of it because a group of Japanese tourists were totally blocking my view, but I could sort of make out her general outline.) I have to say that seeing my beautiful daughter's head start to come out was, without a doubt, one of the most disturbing images that has ever been tattooed on my brain. I think that whole "beauty of childbirth" thing doesn't really kick in until a snuggly soft blanket is caressing the baby and the daddy is being equally caressed by 20 mg of Valium.

🦴 🦴 🦴

So, I'm there, holding Melissa's hand, offering words of encouragement that probably sounded more like what they really were: whimpers of unconditional surrender.

"Here she comes," the doctor announces.

Daddy. I become "Daddy," right now.

In a rush of fluids and blood this person who, up to this point, has been nothing more than a prominent bump in our bed, enters the world with much fanfare and hoopla, none of it provided by me. I didn't move. I didn't know what to do or say.

"Would you like to cut the umbilical cord?" the doctor asks me.

I must have said yes, because before I knew it I had a pair of surgical scissors in my hand and I was attempting to cut the cord that technically was still keeping my daughter alive. The cord was wet, soft, and gray. I had to try a couple of times before the scissors bit through it.

With a muted snip my daughter became her own person.

But, before I even had a chance to form a sentient thought a nurse took the baby from the doctor's hands and whisked her away to an area in the room where they began to clean her up.

"Go ahead, go look at your daughter," Melissa instructs me.

I slowly shuffle my way toward what has quickly become Baby Girl Central.

Count fingers and toes.

I seem to recall reading this somewhere, or it had been drummed into my head from countless movies and television shows that show new dads doing exactly that. *Hey!* I'm *a new dad; I think I'll do exactly that.*

I count. Twice. And I get ten both times. I'm really happy about that because that means my daughter is healthy, and because math has never been my strong suit. I sometimes catch a glimpse of Emmy's fingers and toes today, and I remember when they were more like the promise of fingers and toes; powder-scented suggestions of appendages.

"Eight pounds, five ounces," one of the baby crew calls out.

"Is that a little light?" I mumble to nobody in particular.

"Nope, perfect for her length, which is…twenty inches," another person announces and then writes on a form.

I look at the stub of what was, up until one pair of shiny scissors ago, her umbilical cord. It looks so harsh. So abrupt. I wonder if it hurt her. The wiping, measuring, gauging, foot printing, and wrapping continues until one of the women presents me with my daughter. She tells me how to hold my arms. I have never concentrated so hard in all my life on the position of my arms. I remember how long the process took, amazed that there even *was* a process to holding your baby. My motions so deliberate, each second so irreplaceably precious.

I carefully walked over to Melissa and showed her our daughter. She was covered with sweat, obviously exhausted and deeply, hopelessly in love with the young lady that we now cradled between us. As I stood there numb and staring into my daughter's tiny blue eyes, and as my wife was being, shall we say, sewn back up, I felt something shift. *Shuffle* is probably a better word. Everything in my life that I felt was important, that I was *convinced* was important, got rudely and permanently shoved down one spot at that exact moment. There was a new number one, and her place at the top was for life. My life. Her life. Our lives.

That's when time, at least in relation to a lot of things, became something to relish and not something to beat. Since that very memorable, remarkable day, the baby with the blue eyes has turned into an eleven-year-old person who makes me smile more than should be legal. And those blue eyes still melt my heart on a daily basis. And, as you would imagine, Emmy's fingers lost their baby stubbiness long ago. I already see them beginning to exceed her grasp. Which is why, when I hug her, I tend to let my arms remain as long as possible. My grasp of my baby is being tested by time. I always joke with Emmy and tell her that when she was born, I was able to hold her in just one arm. Now two are barely up to the task.

You'd be surprised as to how many deer there are in New Jersey. You can see them walking in our yard, jumping across the street, and spreading their little deer pellets all over God's creation. Baxter loves rolling in deer poop; all the dogs do. But, whereas Baxter and Molly will rush to find the freshest pile, Maya will wait until Baxter and Molly have had their turn and then slowly walk over, flip onto her back, and leisurely roll back and forth, back and forth. There is no sense of urgency, she just rolls and, as a postrolling bath will attest to, soaks it all in.

What's the rush? I suppose that's what I take away from Maya's slow, deliberate approach to life. Then again, she doesn't have the demands put upon her that I have put upon me. It's not as easy a trick for us humans to simply lie back and let time have its way with us. Our knee-jerk reaction is to fight time, to beat it, to bend it to our will. The great irony, of course, is that in the end, *time* beats *us*. Without fail. Which leads me to believe that Maya's approach is probably the right way to go. Oh, sure, it's not based on focus group testing or years of scientific study. But, that's why it seems so appropriate. She has no agenda, no ulterior motive. She does what she does because it feels good and right and pure. And good, and right, and pure, at this point in my life, sounds good enough for me.

I have to be on a plane next week. I will rise before the alarm. I will arrive three hours before takeoff. And, before I leave the house in the dark of early morning I will go into my daughter's bedroom, stroke her hair, kiss her head and whisper, "Daddy loves you."

And I will linger.

Dachshund Life Lesson #13

Time moves fast enough on its own— don't help it.

14

Death by Kisses

There are some people, such as myself, who enjoy the occasional chocolate treat. And then there are others who put chocolate up there with such other basic necessities like air, water, food, and Xanax. The ones who, when praying, face toward the Milk Chocolate Mecca of Hershey, Pennsylvania. When I'm in the mood for something chocolate my tastes are pretty pedestrian, requiring neither a Swedish chocolatier nor a second mortgage on my house. I like Hershey's Kisses. I know there's not much to them, but I like their simplicity. I like the consistency of their taste. And, for some weird reason, I like peeling those little foil wrappers. What can I say? When the periodic chocolate yen hits, I love them little Kisses, which should not be confused with the kisses from a little dog. For if you do, don't say I didn't warn you.

As I said already, Molly is a big fan of licking, which, in my mind and pretty much everyone else's mind, is a dog's version of kisses. They can't pucker, so they lick. But Molly's licks go beyond the norm. It's not that her licks are any wetter than Baxter's licks, nor does she have an especially long or overly abrasive tongue. What makes Molly's licks so unique is the intention of her licks.

The dog wants to kill me.

I'm not being paranoid, so don't even go there. I'm telling you right now that Molly wants to take me out. With extreme prejudice. And she's surmised that the best way to do that is one lick at a time. If Molly is within a foot of my face, she will find a way to bombard me with her tongue, and I don't use that word by accident. She pokes and darts and jabs and smacks and flicks. Affection? This is an oral assault. I turn and toss my face to no avail. Everywhere I look I'm staring smack into a little black eye, and in it I always see the cold reflection of murder.

But Matt, you already said that Baxter licks you every morning, what's the difference? I'll tell you, dear reader, exactly the difference. Baxter *does* lick me every morning, but I know that Baxter will eventually grow bored with me: If I don't put an end to it, Molly will lick me until one of two things happen: either she collapses from exhaustion, or the skin is no longer on my face. If Molly had the ability to pack a light lunch and make a day of licking my face, she would. The first minute is tolerable; the second is irritating, the third, I'm pretty sure, is probable cause in thirty-six states.

I know what you're thinking: *She's a little Dachshund; just move her out of the way.* You're right; she's a little Dachshund. Ever hear of "good things come in small packages"? Well, apparently, so does obsessiveness bordering on cruelty. And, I feel kind of weird admitting this, but when she goes all licky on me she kind of creeps me out. Remember that Hitchcock movie *The Birds*? Well, from the first time I saw that movie as a kid up until this very moment, that movie has freaked me out! Just the sound of flapping wings gives me the willies. To this day, when I go into the pet store to buy dog food or get the dogs groomed, I look at those parakeets with unease. All of that twitching and the tweeting, and those doll-like eyes—*ugh*—I get goose bumps just thinking about it. That's what goes through my mind when Molly is hunting and pecking me. She's a crow with a collar and an oral fixation. I often imagine looking outside and seeing hundreds of Dachshunds sitting on the grass, on the hood of the car, on the roof, in the street. And all of that maniacal panting.

I know she's showing affection, I do. I get it. I guess Molly's just another reminder of how you can sometimes hurt the ones you love, especially when you don't mean to. Although, if there's one thing a twelve-pound Dachshund that woefully underestimates her tongue's pounds-per-square-lick quotient has taught me, it's that *not* showing signs of affection can be even *more* painful.

🦴 🦴 🦴

Okay, so, apparently I'm emotionally unavailable.

Makes it sound as if my emotions would be happy to speak with you, however, they're unavailable at the moment. Would you like to leave a message for my emotions or do you want to call back? My emotions *are* available; they've *always* been available. They come out when they feel like coming out. It's not my fault that my emotions deem most people and events not worthy of their presence. What can I say? My emotions are not easily impressed. And the older I get the more that seems to increase. It's not *all* of my emotions that don't want to come out to play with any great frequency. Frustration, anger, disappointment, jealousy, insecurity, impatience, and negativity are out and about in plain sight almost every day, reporting for duty like all good soldiers. But, they're loitering around for a very good reason: necessity.

One of the best pieces of advice I ever received was when I was back in high school and I was taking my driver's education class over the summer. After slipping behind the wheel of what was probably something along the lines of a Plymouth K-Car, or some kind of similarly benign vehicle, my teacher told me and my three fellow students something that comes to mind pretty much every time I leave my home: "Whenever you get behind the wheel of a car, I want you to drive as if everyone else on the road is an asshole." I remember these words for two reasons. First, it was the first time I ever heard a teacher curse—and it was awesome; second, everyone else on the road actually *is* an asshole. And what thirty-odd years have also taught me, sadly, is that the assholes aren't content to just stay within the little white lines. They're everywhere.

They're behind me in the line at Target trying to determine if their thirty-seven items somehow disqualifies them from standing in the ten-items-or-less line. They're in front of me at the traffic light, apparently waiting for a more pleasing shade of green instead of the shade that is currently in use in approximately six million traffic lights nationwide. They're the toll-booth taker who insists on taking out his or her frustration over the sudden realization that he or she made a terrible career choice, by treating me as if I'm not even there, as if the coins are magically appearing in thin air and tossing themselves into the change basket. And they're every person that seems to forget that what makes a story interesting is determined not by the person telling the story, but by the person listening to the story. I've tried people, really, really tried. Every day I give people the benefit of the doubt and I am, ultimately, left wanting.

So, you see, what many perceive as me being a bit of a negative, pessimistic prick isn't a conscious choice that I've made: it's a result. It's an asshole by-product. And the truth is that I'm used to it. I'm perfectly fine with leaving not so well enough alone, with the world on one side and me on the other. What concerns me more is that on many occasions my anger against the world has gotten in the way of me letting those people I *do* care about know that I *do* care about them. Or worse. And let's face it: my inner circle isn't exactly what you would call standing room only.

🦴 🦴 🦴

Feigning interest is not really my strong suit, which is unfortunate, seeing as it's one of the key tools in both a husband's and a father's toolbox. But if I was issued it when I first became a husband, I seem to have lost it somewhere between "I do" and onesies. And, to make matters worse, I have a terrible poker face. I'm very bad at concealing anger, annoyance, and dissatisfaction, which unfortunately, are the emotions that without fail show up for work bright and early each and every day.

"Can't you at least pretend that you're listening to me?"

Melissa has asked me on many occasions after I've long tuned out something she was saying.

Hmmm? What'd you say, babe?

Feigning interest, pretending to listen, or anything even remotely resembling paying attention—if I'm not *actually* concerned with what is being said or what is happening—just isn't in my wheelhouse. And, it's not that I'm not *aware* that I'm not pretending to care—I'm totally aware: I just suck at it. Oh, sure, sometimes I'll do a little tap-dancing, apologize, and ask Melissa to repeat what she said so I can then force-engage myself into the conversation that I can only hope will be both brief in duration and benign in nature. Am I wrong to behave this way to the wife that I love dearly? Yep. Do I attempt to change my behavior? Sometimes. Do I succeed when I do? Rarely. I feel bad when I make my wife feel like I don't care about what she has to say or how she feels about something. But, most of all, I hate it when I make her doubt my love for her. And, again, it happens more than it should.

🦴 🦴 🦴

Hallmark cards truly make me gag. When I see the Kay Jewelers commercial around the holidays or Valentine's Day, I want to throw my shoe at the television. I hate when marketing companies attempt to define for me what love is. The fact that I work for a marketing company is an awkward coincidence. But if I see another Cialis commercial, featuring a perfectly coiffed, middle-aged couple holding hands while sitting in matching bathtubs on a cliff overlooking the Pacific Ocean,

I'm going to throw myself off said cliff. Romance is fine, but when mist-covered roses and four-hour erections enter the picture, I'm afraid I have to draw a big, fat, tumescent line. Call me a romantic realist.

Fortunately, Melissa is also a realist when it comes to stuff like that. But that doesn't mean that she'll turn up her nose on a dozen long-stemmed or, for that matter, a four-hour erection (the woman is only human). And that's sort of where I screw things up: the choices I make in expressing my love for her. I think I'm showing her every day how much she means to me. I think the disconnect is that *she* isn't seeing what *I'm* seeing, for example.

On Monday and Thursday evenings I take out the garbage. She doesn't ask me to take out the garbage. I take it upon myself to drag the cans to the curb. To me, that is a romantic gesture. I'm not one of those people who believe that men should be in charge of all refuse responsibility simply because we are the proud owners of two testicles. I'm all for equal rights. Hey, anytime anything in our house breaks, which is often, it's not me who goes to get the "regular" screwdriver and the one that has that crisscrossy shape, it's Melissa—which is probably for the best when you consider that I just referred to a Phillips-head screwdriver as the one with that "crisscrossy" shape. So, I see taking the garbage out as not just a gesture of municipal responsibility, but also a genuine gesture of love.

At first you wouldn't think that three small Dachshunds could eat so much food, but every few weeks we have to go to the store and purchase a fifty-pound bag of kibble. Fifty pounds! That has to be picked up and placed in the shopping cart, picked up and placed in the trunk of the car, picked up and placed in the garage and then, picked up and emptied into a large plastic, airtight container. My wife has a bad back. I'm not going to allow her to pick up that big heavy bag when my perfectly good back is standing right there. Okay, I wouldn't say my back is perfect. I have my issues as well, but, you know, I'm probably in better shape to lift that tremendous dead weight than my wife with her bad back. It's not like she has a titanium rod in there supporting her vertebrae or something. But still, every two weeks I pick up that bag and dump its contents into the plastic canister, while Melissa helps guide the flow of food into the container with her hand. Because, apparently, gravity isn't doing a good enough job. But the point I'm making is that I lift that bag so my wife doesn't have to, plain and simple! I love her, and no wife of mine is going to struggle with a fifty-pound bag of dog food as long as I'm around. Even though my back also...okay... never mind. She's not lifting the bag—end of story. Godiva chocolates, my ass!

Rain, sleet, hail, gloom of night? Not for my wife. She will not run the risk of tripping over the cracks in the driveway nor the icy patches when the winter winds blow. Uh-uh. Every day I tend to my appointed round and traverse the thirty or so yards that separate us from our mail. Armed with bills and an acre's worth of catalogs, I enter the house and place our mail on the kitchen island for my wife to review at her leisure. You can keep your sappy poems and scrapbook of memories. Love means never having to ask, "Babe, did you get the mail?" And my baby doesn't. Ever!

And, every evening, before Melissa's sawing wood and I'm knee-deep in a good book, I secure each and every door. That's three locks dutifully slammed home without her having to ask me, and so, I ask you: Is that not the epitome of love? Of romance? Ensuring the safety of the ones you love? I can see by the dubious look on your face that while all of my actions may be well-meaning and, perhaps, even a little noble, they are not what one would term romantic. Relax. I'm not really surprised by your reaction, mainly because that's Melissa's reaction. While she appreciates all of the more mundane things that I do, I guess a dozen red roses still come out smelling sweeter than me. And, to make matters worse, Emmy isn't a roses kind of girl.

🦴 🦴 🦴

Like her mother, Emmy is a sensitive Scorpio. She's also a bit of a drama queen. That's a bad combination for a daddy like me who often forgets just *how* sensitive and how alike she is to, say, Susan Lucci, when Erica Kane was in her prime. It doesn't take much to bruise her feelings. A poorly chosen word, a questionable tone of voice, or a stern face that somehow, after Emmy's done interpreting it, has suddenly morphed to angry.

"Daddy, remember that kid I told you about in my class yesterday?" she asks me one early evening.

"Emmy, you tell me about some kid in your class every day, it's hard for Daddy to remember which one you're talking about. Can you be a bit more specific?"

"Dad! The kid who was wearing the hat? *With the shirt?*"
She's exasperated with me. There's nothing more frustrating
to an eleven-year old than a father who just doesn't get it.

"Emmy," I say a little too forcefully, "I've been on confer-
ence calls today, I've been trying to string three sentences
together that have refused to be strung together, and you want
me to remember some random kid with a *hat* and a *thing*?
Why don't you just ask me if I remember the kid with the legs
and the head?"

Her lips begin to turn down. She glances at Melissa. The
legs of her chair squeak in protest against the tile as she leaves
the kitchen table.

"Emmy, I'm sorry, come here." My words trail her up the
stairs where a moment later I hear the click of her bedroom
door.

"She's upset," Melissa unnecessarily informs me.

"Ya think?"

"Hey, it's that sarcasm that just chased your daughter
upstairs. Keep it up and I'm going to join her."

Sigh.

"Babe, some days I just don't have the energy to pretend I
care about yet another kid with a backpack."

"Hat!"

"Whatever! You're missing the point. Look, I spend the
better part of my day feigning interest about, well, pretty
much everything. By the time Emmy comes home I've got
nothing left."

"I know, but, you have to remember that she's your daughter and she wants to share things with you, even if it's something that you're not even remotely interested in, including a kid who, apparently, possesses an amazingly memorable hat."

"So what you're saying is that I can't ever get a break?"

Melissa fixes me with the stare that can freeze water.

"No. What I'm telling you is that that girl upstairs *is* your break. So, when you're having a shitty day remember that the best part of your day gets home from school at 3:30. I suggest you go up there right now and remind yourself of that."

My next sigh is not one of frustration: it's of regret. I head upstairs.

"Bobo, can I come in?"

"Okay."

"Emmy, I'm sorry. I had a lousy day and I took it out on you and I didn't mean to do that. I'm sorry."

"Daddy, I understand that you had a bad day, but I was just trying to tell you something and you made me feel bad about it. So, ya know, I feel kinda bad."

"I'm sorry baby, don't feel bad, let *me* feel bad, because it was my fault. Okay? I'm really sorry."

It's at that point I feel a somewhat damp, rosy check next to mine in a sign that all, at least for the moment, is forgiven.

"Okay, so Daddy, can I tell you about this kid—"

"—with the *hat*, right?" I happily interject.

Two quick minutes later I discover why my daughter was so eager to tell me about the kid with the hat: it was a Pittsburgh Steelers hat. I *love* the Pittsburgh Steelers. And so, she thought I'd enjoy hearing about the kid with the Pittsburgh

Steelers hat. A moment later, I am the one with the damp cheek.

❧ ❧ ❧

My girls deserve better. And not just when I remember to try to *do* better. Of all the people that they come in contact with, people who will end up hurting them in some way, shape, or form, one of those people should never be me. Ever. So I've been making a concerted effort to listen more, really listen. To give more spontaneous, longer-lasting hugs. I give Melissa unexpected massages on a back that bears just as many burdens as I do, and usually without as much complaining. And, whenever the Pittsburgh Steelers are playing, the first and last person I ask to sit by my side is the little girl who remembered what her father all too often forgets, namely, that when you love someone you should let them know, in ways both large and small.

And, speaking of small, I'm afraid Molly might be a lost cause. I might just have to accept the fact that I live with a Dachshund that lives to lick. And, while it might cost me portions of my epidermis and, quite possibly—in the long run—my life, I've learned another valuable lesson from her. Never assume that the ones you love *know* they are loved. Tell them. Show them. Remind them even when you think you don't need to. It's one of those things you just can't have too much of, kind of like licks from a Dachshund. Or, Kisses from Pennsylvania. In the end, both are pretty sweet.

Dachshund Life Lesson #14

Emotions are complicated; kisses are pretty straightforward.

15

Do You Smell What I See?

What its prominence suggests, and what all science confirms, is that the dog is a creature of the nose.
Alexandra Horowitz, *Inside of a Dog*

When it comes to the sense of smell we humans stink.

At least when compared to dogs.

Whereas humans have about six million scent receptor sites lining the insides of our noses, dogs have on average over 200 million. What that ultimately means is that a dog's nose is doing much more than just smelling. It's detecting, identifying, informing, measuring, mapping, interpreting, interrogating, convicting, and judging. While some breeds of dogs are known for having exceptional eyesight and others for possessing amazing hearing, *all* dogs experience the world, first and foremost, through their noses. Even when they're seemingly asleep, the occasional twitch tells you that their nose is always on duty. I'm fond of saying that Maya's hearing is so acute, that she can hear a mouse farting. Truth is, it would have to be an unusually large mouse for Maya to hear it fart, but if there *were* a giant, gassy rodent in our basement, and I'm really hoping there isn't, I'm pretty sure Maya's nose would know it before anyone else's.

Even as a kid, one of the first dog facts I remember hearing was that if a dog's nose is wet and cold to the touch, then that dog was in good health. I also heard that a dog's saliva was antiseptic, however, after much discussion I failed to convince my mother that a few licks from King was just as good as a couple of stinging squirts of Bactine. Consequently, after we got King, I would spend a lot of time observing, touching, and palpating his nose, searching for any unusual drops in temperature or moisture content. I was a prepubescent ear, nose, and throat doctor sans the ears and the throat. That's how much emphasis was put on that damn nose. It was like we owned a nose that just happened to be attached to a hundred-pound body. It was only when I was an adult that I realized that a dog's nose could do much more than simply tell you when he was under the weather.

It's more than a little amusing when, after I open the front door, all three dogs make a beeline for the grass and, almost immediately, find a particular spot worth investigating with their noses. They all approach the process the same way. Initially, they'll take a few hesitant steps toward the spot and hover their noses a few inches above that spot. Then, very slowly, they'll lower their noses until they're as close as they can get to touching the ground without actually touching it. Their nostrils begin to methodically inhale deeply and then noisily exhale, often disturbing the ground enough to create a quick puff of dirt. If there's ever a time when you can look at a dog and see its wheels spinning, it's when they're using that nose of theirs. There they stand, muzzles pointed directly at the ground as their scent receptors go to work on detecting and deciphering all kinds of information: a squirrel stopped here to eat a nut, a deer chose this spot a couple of weeks ago to paw at the soil, and exactly twelve hours ago, the beagle from across the street took an unauthorized piss. There I am, an idiot human with my woefully inadequate nose, while three Dachshunds are—quite literally—absorbing an entire world.

What must it feel like to have the ability to be that attuned to something? To take something as commonplace as smelling and have it tell you so much more than simply what's for dinner. You sometimes hear stories of an old dog going blind, but armed with its amazing sense of smell it can still navigate its surroundings. Its nose literally replaces its eyes. It's almost as if they can smell the memories of where their food bowl used to be, which sofa cushion offered their old bones the softest place to rest, and where a comforting, welcoming hand can still be found.

Molly's nose looks like the dot at the bottom of a long, exclamation point of a snout. It certainly doesn't look like much. But, if there's one thing that a dog's nose proves, it's that looks can be deceiving. Which, I guess, is why dogs look to their noses for truth and answers. To a dog, smelling is believing. And what I discovered is that that's never more so than during winter.

Winter is, by far, my favorite season. Not just because of the way it makes the world look, but also the way it makes the world sound: quieter. Snow seems to muffle the loudness and harshness of the world; it tempers its problems. Several inches of the white stuff is nature's way of telling the world to "SSSSHHHH!" At least until the next warm spell. To my ears, there is nothing more profoundly wonderful than listening to the inimitable sound of snow falling at night. It's a climatological time-out. But let's be realistic: winter is at its most beautiful, its most moving, when viewed from inside the comfort and safety of a warm house. After all, winter isn't all tiny marshmallows in your hot chocolate and glowing coals in the hearth. Winter comes with costs, some that can be gauged by the thermostat and others measured by muscle.

There's the shoveling and the scraping; the dead batteries and broken tree limbs; the fender benders and the flu. It means days of aching backs and the incomparable sensation of snow falling down the nape of your neck, the result of a well-aimed snowball. All of this makes my love of winter a great irony, for while it is a season that seems to lend itself to contemplative relaxation, it is the season where relaxing is a hard thing to come by. It's the season that requires the most planning and the greatest degree of vigilance. But if winter is hard on me, it's even harder on Dachshunds.

Dachshunds have a reputation for disliking rain and deservedly so. It's not unusual to see Melissa standing on the grass in the middle of a summer squall, golf umbrella perched on her shoulder, as she attempts to provide Molly with shelter from the storm. Nine times out of ten Molly will simply stare at Melissa, wondering why she insists on going out in such inclement weather. Maya's the same. Baxter is the only one who will even consider going out in a heavy rain to answer the call of nature, but even then, he expedites the process so he can get back into the house as soon as possible. Nope, the guys are not fans of rain. And then there is snow.

There is nothing more entertaining than watching the dogs tear out through the front door to encounter the first heavy snow of the season. Although it is a journey short on duration. Dachshunds just aren't built for snow. Any accumulation of more than a couple of inches creates a real impediment to the dogs either doing their business or simply just walking. They literally can't navigate the landscape. This has led us to creating a designated spot on the front lawn where the dogs can quickly get to so they can take care of business and head right back inside as quickly as possible. It even has a name: the poop patch.

Winter has not officially arrived when I see the first snowflake, or hear the sound of the garbage truck spreading salt on the roads, or even when my L.L. Bean snow boots make their yearly appearance—it's when I hear the telltale sound of aluminum shovel meeting snow-covered grass. Kind of a *crrsshhhh*.

In the early morning after the first heavy snow, when the streets are unplowed and the stars are still hanging in the sky like astral night-lights, Melissa makes her way to the garage to collect a shovel. She then heads to an area just outside the front door where she carves out what looks like a sloppy circle, approximately twenty feet in diameter. And, for the rest of the winter, that circle will become even sloppier, churned into a morass of dog poop, mud, and what used to be grass. I feel so bad for my front yard. Every winter it must wonder to itself, *What the hell did I do to be on latrine duty again?*

🦴 🦴 🦴

Once the poop patch has been carved into existence, it awaits its visitors. With a pink promise starting to peak over the eastern horizon, Baxter, Maya, and Molly tear out into the patch, each quickly selecting a choice spot where they relieve their bladders and bowels, after which they head right back into the house, leaving three sodden pools and three quickly freezing piles of dog turd. If the temperature stays cold it's not long before the poop patch begins to resemble a sort of fecal Stonehenge. But the problem with the poop patch is that it will quickly be covered again with another layer of snow. And so, Melissa will once again head out into the crackling cold of January to play her winter's role of patch janitor. But to be honest with you, I think she sort of likes tending to it. I think she likes the satisfaction that comes from battling nature, even if it's battling nature to create what is, literally, a shit hole. There also isn't much she wouldn't do for the dogs. I've often joked that what the dogs really need come wintertime is a network of tunnels dug throughout the yard, thereby giving them not just a chance to answer the call of nature but also the opportunity to get a little exercise. An underground Habi-trail for Dachshunds, if you will. I could swear I saw Melissa working out the logistics of excavating just such a thing in her head, but to date nothing's happened. I think she's still in the planning stages.

Just so you know, I don't *make* Melissa do the poop patch; it just sort of happened naturally. I'm usually responsible for shoveling the front walk, spreading salt on the brick pavers, scraping windshields, and doing a lot of the more heavy snow-related lifting. Like many things between husbands and wives, our winter routine seems to have divided itself through natural selection. I got scrapers and salt; Melissa got shit. God, I love that woman!

#

The sun is now starting to peek through with purpose. Recently shed boots lay wet and chilled by the front door. The dogs are, once again, enveloped in several layers of blankets and snuggling against each other, searching for the kind of warmth that can come only from the body of another living creature. I gladly recline into the corner of the sofa, where I have a clear view of the world outside the big picture window. Soon enough I hear the comforting sound of Baxter snoring, which somehow always makes me feel more at ease, more at home. I quickly grab one of the tattered blankets that the dogs seem to have missed and pull it up to my chin. It's just before 7:00 a.m. The house is still quiet. My eyes close. This feels good. At least, until I start thinking.

❦ ❦ ❦

I find it hard to shut down my mind. I wish it had an on/off switch because simply willing it to turn off just doesn't seem to work. It never has. The more I try to go blank, the more the major and the mundane make their presence known. It's like my brain is on a continuous loop, a mental Muzak station playing such hits as "I don't really like my job," "We really have to sell this house," "That damn truck needs another oil change," "The basement needs to be cleaned out," "I can't forget to book that Boston trip," and everyone's favorite, "Did I remember to lock the doors?" It's exhausting mentally and physically. I can feel my thoughts bearing down on my neck, my shoulders, and my back. And, it's not even like I'm thinking deep, worthwhile thoughts, like how to cure cancer or how to make the airplane boarding process go smoother. My mind is filled with junk, the flotsam and jetsam of life: a never-ending to-do list of errands, chores, and niggling thoughts. I know my time would be better spent getting a good night's sleep or simply enjoying whatever I'm doing at a given moment, but try telling that to my mind. Seriously, try, 'cause it sure isn't listening to me. Maybe *you'll* have better luck.

❦ ❦ ❦

"Whatcha thinking?" Melissa asks me yet again.

"Nothing," I respond automatically.

The truth is a lot closer to everything. I'm literally thinking of everything.

There I sit, a winter wonderland outside my window, and I'm thinking of nonsense. This would be a perfect opportunity to just lie down and stare into the snow globe that is just a few feet away. To just unplug. Problem is, I don't unplug. In fact, I do the exact opposite. I keep plugging in more mental extension cords, filling my mind with clutter and obstacles. I sit, I dwell, I stew, I worry, I consider, I debate, I ponder, and I get myself into such a state that trying to do anything *but* think is completely pointless.

Baxter slowly pads his way into the living room, unworried and certainly unburdened of any serious issues. The only sounds are his black nails tapping against the wood floor. *Clack-clack-clack-clack.* It's like living with the world's slowest flamenco dancer. It's now midday. The sun has broken through the clouds and is pouring through the picture window, dressing the floors and walls with streaks of gold. It's at this moment that I see Baxter do something that I've never seen him do before, or at least something that I've never noticed him do before: he sniffs the wall.

On any given day Baxter will sniff pretty much every conceivable surface and item in the house: furniture, shoes, laundry, plastic bags from the market, old rawhide chips, rugs, wastebaskets, and every crotch within reach. But I've never seen him sniff the wall. He stands there for a few seconds, seemingly deep in thought. Strange. Baxter doesn't have deep thoughts—he's Baxter. He turns his head and looks at me, the sunlight turning his dark brown eyes to a shade of something just short of amber. It's at that moment that I come to an odd realization. Baxter wasn't just sniffing the wall: he appeared to be sniffing the sunlight, as if it were a tangible thing. But, that can't be right. It's sunlight. There's nothing to smell. Baxter begins walking toward the big, blue pillow that rests on the floor next to the sofa. As he walks, his nose points toward the floor and traces the same beam of sunlight that he discovered on the wall. Like a short, fat drunk walking a white line, Baxter follows the beam of sunlight right to the pillow. After a couple of lazy turns he plops down right in the middle of the pillow, which just happens to be where the ray of sunlight seems to be at its brightest. The light cuts across his muzzle an inch or two shy of his eyes. In a matter of moments, his eyelids are closed, and the sun is now a warm, white slash against his jet-black fur. He takes in a deep breath and exhales loudly. His ribs slowly rise and fall at a familiar pace, telling me that he is asleep.

A few moments later, both Maya and Molly come in from the kitchen and perform the same remarkable ritual with the sunlight on the wall. Both of them also come to rest on the big, blue pillow, where they carve out spaces among the pillow's creases and Baxter's bulk. There they rest, warm, safe, and seemingly, incredibly content. As I stare at what is now, in essence, a pile of dog, I notice that the sun is slowly, almost imperceptibly moving across their bodies.

Sunlight?

Sunlight!

You know, the sun often gets a bad rap. People bitch and moan when it's hot. They complain when too much sun burns their skin. They whine when the sun causes a heat wave, killing grass, plants, and crops. And over the past couple of decades, the sun has been the fall guy for an array of skin diseases brought on by too much sun exposure, namely skin cancer. But maybe we should all remember that the sun also does something for us that, I think, sort of balances out a lot of the bad things. What was that thing that the sun does again? Oh, right—*it enables life*!

That's right—without the sun we would cease to exist. Our little old planet would be a cold, lifeless ball. Besides, who holds the gun to your head when you insist on basting yourself in oil and bake your epidermis until it's something akin to bison leather? Who *is* that person? Oh, and who tells you to go outside, leaving the air-conditioned splendor, to sweat your nuts off when the temperature hits one hundred degrees? Oh, that's right, nobody! You are your own worst enemy. So, before you start going on and on about the sun this and the sun that, remember you're only here because of the sun. Oh, and as if giving us a planet to live on isn't enough for you, sunlight does a lot of other great things for us unappreciative humans, such as:

- strengthening the cardiovascular system
- normalizing blood pressure and blood sugar
- increasing metabolism
- aiding in weight loss
- ensuring proper function of liver and kidneys
- improving digestion

- supplying us with vitamin D, which keeps our bones and our immune system strong

Plus, one of the major health benefits of sunlight is that it increases the production of endorphins and serotonin in your brain, which soothes nerves and leaves you with a renewed sense of well-being, thereby helping to prevent anxiety and depression. Looking at the dogs I can believe it.

They seem utterly relaxed, loose, and without a care in the world. Granted, being dogs, they don't really have much on their plates, even under the worst of circumstances. A tennis ball stuck under the sofa pretty much qualifies as a catastrophe. But right now they are at peace, seemingly separated from any thoughts, large or small. As I've been looking at the dogs I suddenly notice that the sun has progressed to the sofa. The edge of the sunbeam is nearly touching my sock. I decide to do as the dogs do. I decide to submit to the sun. Of course, I've subjected myself to the sun's rays for years, shooting many, many times for a golden bronze while usually winding up with red-broiled. But this is different. This is sunbathing for medicinal purposes, maybe even emotional purposes.

I lay my head down on the sofa pillow, clasp my hands across my stomach, and close my eyes. While I know that it's eighteen degrees outside, I feel a concentrated blade of warmth on my legs. With the exuberance of a slug, it moves to my waist. I keep my breathing slow. I next feel the sun on my folded hands, its muted warmth easing the pain of a couple of arthritic knuckles. Behind my closed eyelids it is brightening. It's getting harder to keep them closed. The sun is touching my chin. It lights my lips. My limbs feel like lead weights. My eyes are flushed with natural sunlight. I know if I open my eyes it will hurt, so I don't. I also don't know what, if anything, I'm gaining by sitting here letting sunlight paint my body. Well, there is one undeniable thing: an overwhelming desire to be still. To remain idle. To cease thinking. And, for a few precious moments, I seem to do exactly that.

🦴 🦴 🦴

While science has proven how a dog's nose functions and what it is capable of, I believe that, as with many things related to dogs, there is much we will never know or completely understand about them. And, truthfully, I like it that way. Let some of the magic of dogs remain just that. After all, I think that's why they're so special to us to begin with. Look, I have zero idea if any of my dogs could actually smell a mouse's fart. *Or* sunlight. But in its welcome rays they found something they wanted, maybe even needed. It's not important that I know what that thing is. What's important is that my dogs taught me a way to find the silence of winter in the warmth of the sun.

Dachshund Life Lesson #15

*Not thinking is
nothing to sniff at.*

16

I'll Wash; You Try.

I once had a rather promising career as a dishwasher.

I was living in Albany, New York, at the time, with my first wife, and we were desperate for money. After searching for something more appropriate for someone with my distinguished upbringing and background, like, say, pizza delivery guy, I had no choice but to walk into a local restaurant and say, "Yes, I'd love to wash dirty dishes." But, here's the thing: I ended up loving washing dirty dishes. Okay, maybe I didn't love it, but I certainly didn't mind it as much as I thought I would.

It was a small, local café, so there was a certain degree of teamwork that helped make you feel as if what you were doing was important. Like it was us against the giant chain restaurants. And, let's face it; my job was integral to the success of the team. And I performed my job accordingly. I took pride in scrubbing the pots; I had total focus every time I had to slide a rack of dirty dishes into the commercial-grade dishwasher. I can still recall that warm, wonderful scent of soapy antisepticness every time that dishwasher door was opened, steam wafting in my face and pride swelling in my heart. I'm serious! I really enjoyed washing dishes. Granted, it's probably not much of a stretch when you consider that I'm a bit of a neat freak to begin with, but still. To this day, whenever I'm in a restaurant, I always cast a fond eye at the busboy clearing my table, or when a swinging door affords me a glimpse of a busy kitchen. And, I'd be lying if I said there weren't some days when I wish my job were still washing dishes. The simplicity of the task and the immediate tangibility of the results are not something to belittle. I was happy washing dishes. But it should come as no surprise that it didn't make me rich. Hell, it barely made me poor! So, my career as a dishwasher ended before it really began. And, not surprisingly, as is often the case, the passage of time has changed me. I now avoid washing dishes. What I once viewed as an almost noble task I now view as a bottom-of-the-barrel chore. Something I avoid like the plague, or, say, like a sink full of greasy, slimy, dirty dishes.

Fortunately, I have a wonderful wife who's willing to do the dishes and a Sears Kenmore Kick-Ass dishwasher to pick up the slack when elbow grease fails to rid us of actual grease. Oh, and I have Baxter.

The fact that Baxter is willing to lick the scraps off all of our plates is not unique. Give most dogs a plate of scraps and they'll lick it. What does make it special is the amount of effort Baxter puts into the task. After he is done with a plate it isn't just clean—it's pristine. It practically shines. Long after anything that can even be considered a remnant of food is gone,

Baxter is still at it, lovingly licking that plate clean of a meal only he, and his nose, can still detect. Even after Molly and Maya have lost interest and moved on to new food opportunities, Baxter sits on the floor with that plate squarely in front of him and cleans the dishes. Even at my once-upon-a-time best, Baxter puts me to dishwashing shame.

But, that's sort of Baxter in a nutshell.

When he does anything, from licking a plate to chewing on a bone to taking a walk, Baxter puts everything into it. There is no quit in him. Ever. And while that often comes back to bite me in the ass big-time, it's a quality that I can't help but admire. Probably because it's so rare to see a person have that degree of commitment to anything. It's inspiring. So, when I see Baxter cleaning a dinner plate I'm seeing much more than my reflection in its now sparkling surface, I'm seeing a lesson that we all, and certainly I, can benefit from: if you're going to do something, you may as well do it to the best of your ability. Unfortunately, in my own case, the chore I most need to tend to is not a stack of dirty dishes, it's a blood relation.

🦴 🦴 🦴

I haven't spoken to my brother Adam in about seven years. Like a lot of broken relationships, money did a lot of the shattering. I had asked if he could lend me a not-inconsiderable sum so I could pay off a long-outstanding debt. He said no problem. He said, "Take as much time as you need to pay me back." I breathed a sigh of financial relief. Two weeks later he called me to say he needed all of the money back—"now!" I took a cash advance on a credit card, thereby negating the aforementioned financial sigh of relief. We haven't spoken since.

But the money was just a part of it. There were years of disappointment that contributed to the current state of our relationship. The money was just the cherry (at 14.9 percent interest, no less) on top.

In any event, I felt betrayed and hurt, and I cut off all communication with him. During those fleeting moments when I consider picking up the phone or sending him an e-mail, I think about what happened and how I felt, and the phone stays mute in its cradle. And the thought passes. But, as I get older, those fleeting moments seem to come back with greater regularity. So I begin to rationalize with myself; it was a long time ago, let bygones be bygones, time is passing by, you don't have a lot of family left, people change, etc. Except, I'm not really sure if people do possess the capacity to change.

He was always the one who required those extra couple of parent-teacher conferences. The one who seemed to get into some mischief when other siblings had the sense not to. My brother isn't and never was what you would call a bad person. He's a good person who made some bad choices. Choices that I—nor my other brother, Steven—would never have made. Were my parents' deaths to blame for that? I don't believe so. Steven and I lost the same parents, and we didn't try to take the easy way out. Genetics? Who the hell knows?

All I know is that at the end of the day, each one of us is responsible for his own actions. Adam is responsible for his. I didn't approve of his actions. I couldn't understand his choices, and so our relationship remains frozen. But even if I did wake up one morning and decide to give him a call, he and I, beyond a lot of awkward chitchat, would have nothing of consequence to speak about. After rehashing memories, and you're left with the moment at hand, what do you say? Because Adam and I are as different as night and day. All three of us are.

Melissa has said to me, on many occasions, how she can't believe the three of us come from the same parents. She's not the first one to say that, and it's hard to argue against it.

I am as introverted as Steven is extroverted. Adam is as impulsive as I am cautious and calculating. I can assure you we would be unable to agree on a favorite movie, television show, or author. I sometimes see other siblings around each other, and I can easily tell that they're related. There's a certain shorthand, an easiness and familiarity to the way they interact. If you placed me and my brothers in the same room, brought in a total stranger, and had them speak to us for five minutes, they would have no idea that we were three brothers separated by only six years. It's funny to think of such a scenario. It's *sad* to think of such scenario. Because many years ago we were as close as the butcher, the baker, and the candlestick maker.

🦴 🦴 🦴

I'm not sure who has it.

It was once in a box in my basement but I think at some point I gave it to Steven. Or he might have asked me for it. It's a picture that was taken around 1973, '74. My family and I spent a couple of summers at a bungalow colony in upstate New York that catered to Jewish families. And one of the big events of the summer was a costume party. It was a chance for all of the mothers to show how creative they could be when armed with nothing more than beach towels, Magic Markers, tinfoil, and string. The results were about what you would expect, not that it mattered. I have wonderful memories of it. And I had this one picture.

My mother, in a stroke of design genius, decided that she would leverage the fact that she had three sons by dressing us up as the butcher, the baker, and the candlestick maker of nursery-rhyme fame. I think I was the candlestick maker. I don't remember if we won the contest or won any kind of con- solation prize like " most creative," "best theme costumes," or "best use of masking tape." All I know is that someone took a picture of me, and my brothers at the very height of our butcher-baker-and-candlestick-maker-ness. I was probably eleven or so. You can already see hints of my prepubescent awkwardness rearing its head, which would soon culminate in a mouth full of metal and a raging case of "backne." You can see Steven is, well, chubby. A chubbiness that he will battle off and on for the rest of his life. And in Adam you can see my baby brother. Before poor grades and even poorer choices. I loved that photo, and I don't know what happened to it. I loved it, and not because it's a great photo. I recall it being kind of fuzzy around the edges and yellowing with age. I also recall my mom entombing the picture in Saran Wrap to protect it from getting wet or something or other. One could look at that photo and say that maybe subconsciously she was trying to contain something in that picture. Innocence? The pleasure that comes from seeing your children happy and healthy? Maybe she wanted to lock away the promise of her three boys that she wouldn't live to see turn into three men? I wish she were here to ask.

※ ※ ※

As bad as I feel about not being in contact with my brother, and I do, I feel even worse for my daughter. My parents are deceased. Melissa has no relationship with her mother. Her relationship with her father is, at best, strained. Steven lives in Florida, and while he sometimes talks to Emmy on the phone and sends her gifts on her birthday and Hanukkah, they don't have the kind of close relationship I want them to have. Melissa's sister loves Emmy to pieces, but again geography creates a hurdle. So Emmy doesn't really have a tight circle of family around her. She doesn't have the deep, close relationships with Steven or Melissa's sister like we'd like her to have. In short, Emmy needs all of the relatives she can get. And that kills me, because while my brother Adam has made some bad choices, he has always had the kindest, most giving of hearts.

That's what makes his situation and his choices even more frustrating. How many times I have wondered what could have been, if he were able to marry the good intentions of his heart with some wise choices of his mind.

I'll Wash; You Try.

My Emmy needs kindness. She needs people who will love her and hug her and cherish her for the wonderful, beautiful person that she is. She needs people who will treat her the way my mom and dad would be treating her if they were alive. So I have to ask myself: Is my grudge against my brother hurting my daughter? Am I hurting myself?

🦴 🦴 🦴

At what point is it enough? When is it time to acknowledge that time has healed all wounds? But have those wounds healed? I don't know. I really don't. Besides, even if I went and spoke to my brother and made up with him and buried hatchets and all of that, what, if anything, will I get out of that relationship? We have absolutely nothing in common. I'm sure the passage of time has made that chasm even more distant and daunting. He, like Steven, also lives in Florida. I live in New Jersey. There are probably more reasons I can think of to keep the things the way they are, rather than try to mend the relationship. Except for one: Emmy.

I can't give her grandparents. Perhaps I can give her an uncle. And her uncle another chance. And, maybe, through their relationship, I too can find some peace with my brother. That's a lot to ask for. There's also a lot to gain.

🦴 🦴 🦴

It's a week before Christmas. Hanukkah starts tomorrow night. It seems like the appropriate time to reach out to Adam. Extend some kind of simple gesture toward him. An e-mail probably makes the most sense. It gives me time to craft exactly what I want to say to him. What *do* I want to say to him? *Happy Holidays!* I can't go wrong with that, right? *How's your son?* A son who was born one day before Emmy, and yet the two cousins have never met. That makes me angry. It makes me sad for Emmy. Obviously, this e-mail is going to take a bit of time to compose. That's fine. It won't be the first time that I struggled with writing something. Surely won't be the last. But, I want to do this for Emmy. And myself; of *course* myself. I want to do it for my brother Steven. And for my parents. They've been gone so long I often struggle trying to recall what their voices sounded like. But they had three sons that they loved, and I'm sure they would want the three of us to remain, if not close, at least in touch. Even if we get angry at each other. Even if we went our separate ways, they would want us to always find our way home to each other.

So I think I'll try. The way Baxter tries.

🦴 🦴 🦴

It's the first night of Hanukkah. Melissa made chicken cutlets with potato latkes. At the moment I'm placing my almost-empty plate on the floor my cell phone rings. It's Steven calling to wish Emmy a Happy Hanukkah. I'm glad he remembered. Baxter begins to lap up what's left of the chicken and latkes.

"Daddy, Uncle Steven wants to know if you want to talk to him," Emmy hollers from the other room.

Lick, lick, lick, lick.

"I do, baby. I want to ask him about a picture," I respond,

as I navigate around Baxter and behind Melissa, who's getting a jump on the dishes. Did I mention I love my wife?

"A picture?" Melissa asks me.

"Yeah."

Emmy is about to hand me the receiver when she quickly pulls it back to her ear.

"Bye Uncle Steven, love you!"

I take the receiver from Emmy's hand.

"'Sup brother, happy holiday."

"Thanks. Hey, gotta question for you."

"Shoot."

"Do you still have that picture from the bungalow colony?"

"The costume party one?"

"Yes."

"Sure! Butcher, baker, candlestick maker. Can't lose that one, right?"

"No," I reply, "we can't."

Dachshund Life Lesson #16

You *decide when your plate is clean.*

CHAPTER 17

What's Your Position on Doggie Style?

There, but for the grace of God, go my balls.

That's what goes through my mind whenever I see Baxter attempt to mount Maya, or Molly, or a human leg when available, and try to do that which the veterinarian has made impossible by virtue of a couple of well-placed incisions and snips with a scissor. I feel for him, I really do. He's got the will; he's just no longer in possession of the way.

We brought Baxter to the vet shortly after we got him. According to the literature available, neutering your male dog offers certain physical and emotional benefits. It controls unwanted litters, it prevents testicular cancer, it makes for a pet that is less likely to roam, and it makes for an overall, better-behaved dog. Well, apparently, Baxter never read that literature. Yes, Baxter is unable to procreate. As for the rest of it, let's just say that the literature in the vet's waiting room was not completely accurate.

As far as roaming goes, Baxter, given the opportunity, will walk the earth, not unlike Caine from the '70s TV show

Kung Fu. Baxter's a scent hound. He is ruled by his nose, and as luck would have it, the world totally stinks. Therefore, he will walk, stop and smell, walk, stop and smell. Baxter has a Magellan-like desire to explore the world around him. And, since our yard isn't fenced, when Baxter goes outside, one of us must go outside with him. It sort of gives me an idea as to what prison guards must experience when they're out in the exercise yard with the inmates. But unlike those guards, I've got no barbed wire to work with, no hard time that I can threaten him with, and no firearm. Basically, I've got "Baxter! *No!*" Maximum security it ain't.

Better behavior? If there were a way for me to go back to the vet who neutered Baxter and extract some kind of a refund, based solely on the behavior thing, I would do it. Personally, I think the vet, in a sick, twisted homage to Mary Shelley, took the testes of a Rottweiler and *switched them* with Baxter's already behaviorally challenged nuts. While there's certainly no visual proof to speak of, I can't help but think that something went horribly wrong during the surgery. Baxter isn't just "alive," he's a very bad boy.

And the one who suffers the most from this fact is Maya.

Whenever Baxter recalls that once upon a time, he had the ability to make baby Baxters, he jumps on Maya's back. Or her shoulder. Or her head. While his passion is still there, his aim is for shit. Which makes the whole thing even funnier to watch, except, of course, for Maya. Maya's approaching ten years of age, and back problems are a common ailment in Dachshunds. The last thing she needs is a twenty-five-pound, poorly aligned libido repeatedly slamming into her rib cage.

"Baxter! Get *off* her!" is commonly heard in the house.

And poor Maya, after having to endure the abuse, always looks, more than anything else, embarrassed for Baxter, as if to say, *Wow, that is just really sad.*

And, in a way it is sad. I think that's why men always have a strong reaction, and perhaps reluctance, when it comes to having their dogs neutered. Think about it. You're having your dog undergo a procedure that for all of its touted benefits, is removing the very thing that makes the male of any species distinctly male: the ability to impregnate the female of the species. And when you couple that with the fact that a dog has no idea what's going to happen, and has no say in the matter, it seems like neutering is just about the cruelest thing you can do to a male dog. But I suppose, as the saying goes, the positives outweigh the negatives. Try telling that to Maya.

As I already mentioned, Maya has had a hard life. The very last thing she needs, as she enters her golden years, is a housemate with delusions of romantic grandeur. Or, more likely, just a booty call. But Maya has two things going for her. The first is that there is almost always one of us around when we see Baxter getting ready to get busy. Second, Maya has Molly.

🦴 🦴 🦴

It never fails to amuse all of us when all twelve pounds of Molly intimidates all twenty-five pounds of Baxter. And it is often. If Baxter even looks at Molly's rawhide bone while she's chewing on it, out comes a deep, serious growl from Molly. It's a sound you would think impossible to come out of such a tiny muzzle. It's almost like there's a pit bull hiding behind the couch, and it's throwing its growl. Every time I see it happen it reminds me that the largest dog is not always the "big" dog. There have been instances where Baxter has gotten a little too close for Molly's comfort, and she's taken enough of a nip to leave a mark. What's Maya doing when this is happening? Nothing. She just goes on blissfully chewing her bone. I guess when Molly joined the household she and Maya came to some kind of understanding—namely, that Molly would be Maya's muscle. Which is sort of strange, since Baxter and Molly spend a lot of their time shadowing each other. But, make no mistake: Baxter is always Molly's bitch, and not the other way around. However, Maya's and Molly's fondness for each other is at its strongest when they're sleeping.

I doubt that it's a girl thing. They weren't littermates. Molly is three; Maya is almost ten. It's hard to conceive of any logical kind of reason that they would look for each other when they're looking to catch a nap or settle in for the night. But they do.

You can find them in any one of several body configurations, usually ones that would put a contortionist to shame. But there is always a common trait in their contortions: they are always touching. You would be as likely to find Molly resting her head on Maya's neck as you would Maya doing the same to Molly. Each uses the other's body as a blanket; each often buries her entire face under the other's warm, soft belly fur. They have made snuggling an art form. But I think what makes an even bigger impact on me, and makes their behavior even more amazing, is the way that they deliberately seek each other out.

We keep the dogs in the family room at night. They all sleep on a big, brown, comfy chair that, at one time, I used to enjoy. Baxter is usually the first one to climb up the little Dachshund stairs at the base of chair, where his bulk takes up most of the prime real estate. Next comes Molly, and without a growl or a glance she shoves Baxter out of the way and claims the choicest spot next to one of the chair's arms. Baxter will lay his head down on the chair and start snoring away. Molly? She sits. And she waits. For Maya.

Maya is always the last to arrive. Part of that is age, and part of it is simply another of Maya's inexplicable phobias. But, once in the family room Maya climbs the stairs, steps over Baxter's bulk, and sidles up to Molly. It's then they find a suitable configuration for them, one that best ensures two things: that they are warm and that they are one.

I am reluctant to say that I think that Molly and Maya have each other's backs, because they are dogs. But because they are *my* dogs I'm going to say that they do. Maya and Molly have each other's backs.

I'm going to say it because I sometimes have bad dreams.

🦴 🦴 🦴

I have never fully dealt with the deaths of my parents. And, by fully, I mean I've never dealt with the deaths of my parents. That means that I've never really given each the kind of thought required to accept and cope with their deaths, enabling me to live a rich, full life while still remembering and treasuring the memory of them in a lasting, healthy way. And because I've never done that, part of me is broken. Flawed. Rarely a day goes by that I don't think about my parents. And, when I do, a part of me feels guilty that I've placed their memories, on the day that each died, in a cardboard box and put those boxes in a mental attic, where they've been withering and yellowing with time.

I have never once visited their graves. My father has been dead thirty-one years; my mother twenty-three. Not once. I hardly ever speak of my parents unless they're brought up in some roundabout way—in other words, when I have no choice but to speak of them. I dutifully light memorial candles in their honor on the anniversaries of their deaths and on Yom Kippur, the Jewish Day of Atonement. I light them because I loved them. I light them because I miss them. But do I remember them? Literally, do I recall their voices? How their skin felt against my cheek? How each interacted with me? I'm afraid to admit that the answer might be no. The passage of time isn't just yellowing the boxes that contain their memories; it's yellowing and fading the memories themselves.

Can I find a way to cope better? Sure. Have I? No. Will I? Doubtful. Like so many things in life, I'll come up with some kind of excuse not to. Shortage of time, shortage of money, too busy, too pessimistic about the outcome. After all, I've been a high-functioning human since their deaths. Why bother? Does it make me sad that they're not here? Of course. But has it made me a bad person? No.

What it has made me is a bruised person. I'm certainly not

unique in that respect. The world is filled with people who lost loved ones. Many have and many will deal with that loss better than I did. Some won't have bad dreams about bad days. Others, like me, will. I only hope they have a hand that reaches out for theirs in the dark. One to slow their heart and mind. I hope they have what I have.

＊ ＊ ＊

Melissa knows that the subject of my parents is a sore one. It is for her, too, because she knows how much I miss them and how much it would mean to me for them to meet her and Emmy, and she hurts for me. The pain from my loss is never so pronounced as when seen through my daughter's eyes. I could not give Emmy the honor of meeting my parents, of having them spoil her rotten, which I am sure they would have done. Instead, the only honor I could give her was to bear their names. Emmy's middle name is Paula, my mother's name. My father's name was Paul. They are both there, both remembered. Entwined in name as they were in life. Emmy seems to get a kick out of that fact. She'd get more of a kick if she'd known them.

Every so often, mostly around the holidays, she asks me about my parents. I guess she's taken my vacant stares and quiet moments as signs that I'm thinking of them. She asks me how I celebrated the holidays with my parents. I think she's asking me simply because she wants to hear me talk about her grandparents, which I don't often do. Perhaps, through my words, she can get a sense of what they were like.

I tell her they were both born and raised in Brooklyn. That

they met when they were teenagers. That my dad was in the army. That by the time my mother was twenty-four she had three sons. And that back then, that wasn't unusual. I tell her how they struggled for every dollar. How my dad drove a cab, delivered frozen food to bodegas in the worst parts of Brooklyn and Queens. How he once opened a coffee shop on Twenty-third Street and Seventh Avenue in Manhattan. I tell her how they weren't poor, but they certainly weren't rich. I tell her my parents were smack in the middle of the middle class. I fudge a little.

I tell her how we lived in a two-bedroom apartment. How my brothers and I all slept in the bigger bedroom. And after I was given the small bedroom, my parents slept on the sleeper sofa. And more and more.

I share with her the memory of when my parents bought a house on Long Island. How my brothers and I thought that moving to Long Island was like moving from the city to the country, and in 1974 it almost was. And how we had a backyard and what that meant to us. About the above-ground pool. About riding a bike to school. About vacations to Pennsylvania and how we never flew anywhere because such an extravagance was inconceivable. I tell her that I remember them, my brothers, and me being very happy.

"Even without iPhones?" she asks incredulously.

"*Especially* without iPhones, baby."

"Do you ever have dreams about them?" she asks me.

I tell her I dream about them a lot and that it always makes me happy.

In other words, I lie to my daughter.

This was the most recent one.

We are in the Long Island house. We moved there when I was eleven. Moved out when I was eighteen. Just seven years, and yet that's the place I see when I hear the word *home*. I am in my room. It's small. It has brown carpeting, beige walls, and a matching desk and dresser that my grandmother bought me. The stereo system that my "nanny" also bought me sits on a low coffee table along one wall. I am looking out the window at my parents in the yard. The trees outside my window bring a dimness to my view. They're walking around the aboveground pool. I can just make out snippets of what they're saying:

"...too cold to swim."

"...Here, King! Come!"

I put on a bathing suit and run down the stairs. My hand brushes against the faux brick that my dad put up when we first moved in. There's the front door at the foot of the stairs. The wood paneling. The drop leaf table our aunt gave to my mom. Now I'm in the kitchen. Linoleum. Dark brown cabinets. The dining area that used to be the garage. I push through the storm door onto the large, concrete patio. I remember that the man who sold us the house told us that he put that patio in himself, and how the steel posts are sunk into garbage cans that were filled with concrete. He said the house might blow away some day, but that patio wasn't going anywhere. The concrete feels cold and clammy on the soles of my feet. I'm not wearing a shirt. I have goose pimples all over. I charge onto the grass, looking for my parents. I run around the pool a couple of times, past the tall white flagpole that would fly the American flag every Memorial Day and Fourth of July.

They've vanished.

I hear a sound behind me. It's King. He slowly walks to me. I bend down and bury my face in his thick neck. He smells like grass and mothballs. I hear him panting in my ear. And then he begins to whimper. I don't know how to make him stop. He's in pain. I know he's missing my father. I feel my chest tighten. I have to release this pressure, so I, too, begin to whimper. I let it out of me. My whimpers become cries.

"…It's too cold."

Dad!

"…Here, King! Come!"

Mommy!

"You're okay."

"Daddy!"

"Babe, you're dreaming, you're okay."

"I'm cold."

I wake to find Melissa holding my hand.

"Bad dream?" she asks.

I take a moment to find my voice, to clear it of memory. "Yeah. Bad."

"You're okay, you're fine."

"It was about my parents," I offer.

"What happened?"

"I lost them."

"I know," she says.

She's talking about when they died. She doesn't know I lose them regularly.

"Want me to hold your hand till you fall asleep?"

"Thanks, babe."

"That's what I'm here for."

Here's the thing: I think she's right.

I don't have these dreams a lot. But when I do, they linger like a reluctant scab. But, unlike a scab, I don't pick at the dream, trying to decipher its meaning. I don't have to. It's simple enough. I miss my mom and dad. I regret they're not here to meet my wife and their granddaughter. And the only way I can see them again is through a dream. But as with most dreams, there is always something about them that leaves me unsettled. The kind of unsettled that tags along into my consciousness. I know that time will eventually erode the lingering effects of each dream, but while they remain it feels like a weight. It's then that I wish something that I never would have thought I would ever wish for: I wish for the memory of my parents to trickle away. Because they hurt too much. And I hate myself for thinking that.

I don't know what I would do in those frightful moments

when dream follows me into the edge of reality without Melissa. She calms me. She asks me if I want some cold water or some fresh air. She is my primary safety net and the one person in the world who really knows that the biggest losses in my life never faded to a comfortable presence. She knows that many of my funny quirks stem from nothing even remotely funny. That they are, in fact, pain and tears manifested in everyday habits and behaviors.

When I need soothing, it is her kindness I seek. When I need to feel a reassuring form in the middle of the night, I feel hers. When my memories turn a bit too dark to bear, she is the one that brings me back to the light. When I need someone to lean on—to help me bear my burden—it is Melissa.

I doubt that I have ever thanked her for those strange moments in time, when I see, and then lose, my parents over and over again. Thanked her for filling my hand with hers and my mind with better thoughts. Thank you, babe. I know you know it's a sore subject, but, you should know that it's a subject made a bit less sore by your willingness to listen during those rare times when I feel like speaking about it and by your being there when dreams block words. Thank you.

🦴 🦴 🦴

Occasionally, I'll notice that Molly's body is twitching and she's emitting little squeaky whimpers. If she's within reach, I'll place my hand on her body and gently stroke her fur. It usually stops the twitching and whimpering and banishes the bad dreams. Then again, I have no idea what Molly is dreaming of, or if she dreams at all. I'm assuming it's a bad dream because it looks like something someone who is having a bad dream would do. It looks like something I do.

I also notice that if Molly is laying next to Maya or, as she sometimes does, *on* Maya, she is less likely to have one of her dreams, or is at least less likely to appear *as if* she were having a bad dream. Maybe Maya is Molly's security blanket. Perhaps the warmth of her body and the breath coming out of her nose reassures Molly that she is not alone. That each is only—and always—just a paw's length away.

❧ ❧ ❧

The big brown chair once again awaits its nightly occupants. Here comes Baxter, ready to claim the choicest real estate on the chair. At least temporarily. Molly bounds up the stairs, using her tiny hips to miraculously shove Baxter out of the way. Molly leans against the other arm, turns her head toward the kitchen where she can hear the soft *click-click* of Maya's nails on the tile. Maya climbs the stairs and squeezes next to Molly, and they both proceed to lean against each other. I lazily drape a throw blanket over all three of my dogs and tell them to "go sleep." And then, a breath after I close the light, and while I can still hear them settling their bodies, I offer a final wish—for everyone under my roof:

"Sweet dreams."

Dachshund Life Lesson #17

When you have someone's back, that also includes what's behind them.

CHAPTER 18

Lawn Moaner

"Daddy! Baxter's gonna puke!"

It's a common refrain.

With a common enough clue.

When Baxter is going to vomit he starts licking the floor. Because Baxter doesn't just go ahead and vomit. He puts on a whole big, glitzy regurgitation production. Licking is merely the overture. And he licks with a level of dedication and sense of purpose you usually see in a Dyson vacuum cleaner. And, as with a Dyson, this, too, is quickly going to suck, primarily for me.

For some strange reason, when it comes to Baxter and vomit, I am the chosen one. I don't recall there being a vote, and I certainly can't recall applying for the job. Apparently, some achieve the position of vomitorium attendant and some have the position thrust upon them. I am the latter.

So, the licking overture has finished, the lights go down, the curtain slowly rises and we're treated to Baxter's Stomach Contractions Symphony #2 in G-awful. He stands there with his head pointed somewhere between wall and floor, as his sides expand and compress in a slow rhythm. There's no sound. Just that rolling undulation of his stomach that, while gross, is also sort of hypnotic. It's a bit like watching a belly dancer with a lower GI obstruction.

"Daddy! Do something, he's going to puke," Emmy implores.

"Em, what would you like me to do? Hold his ears away from his mouth? He's done it a million times, babe, just let him do it and he'll feel better, trust me."

"Hon, at least take him outside. Maybe he'll feel more comfortable on the grass," Melissa suggests.

Feel more comfortable?

I've watched Baxter vomit in the house dozens of times. Not once did I ever get the impression that he was, in any way, uncomfortable or inconvenienced. Unlike the humans in the house, Baxter isn't even required to make it to the toilet. All in all, I think he feels quite comfy.

"Babe, take him outside...fast!"

I place both hands under Baxter's heaving stomach and carry him toward the front door, holding him away from my body like he's some kind of ticking bomb that instead of blowing up will blow chunks. I sure don't want to be collateral damage.

I place him on the grass, sides still making like an old black-smith's bellows. It's at this moment when I witness Baxter exhibit a behavior that—up until that point—I had never seen before. He starts eating the grass. And, not just a couple of nibbles and done. For the next ten minutes or so, Baxter does his impression of a John Deere lawn mower. And, I'll tell you, if nothing runs like a Deere, then nothing inhales grass like a Baxter.

"Hon! Can you come out here?" I yell to Melissa through the screen door.

"Did he puke yet?" she yells from inside.

Chomp-chomp-chomp-chomp-chomp.

"He's not quite ready. Come out here!"

Both Melissa and Emmy walk outside.

"He's eating the grass," Emmy says.

"Should he be doing that?" Melissa questions me.

"Who am I, the puke whisperer?"

The three of us stand there for a few seconds watching Baxter eat the grass.

"It's grass, how bad can it be?" I offer.

"Maya eats poop. I can't imagine grass being bad for them, right?" Melissa hypothesizes.

"Exactly. I just wish I knew why he's doing it."

As I utter these words Baxter stops eating the grass and walks over onto the driveway. His sides are moving in earnest now. His whole body starts to tense. He's about to blow. Somewhere in the recesses of my memory, I recall my mom placing her hand on my forehead whenever I threw up in the toilet. When I was a little kid I found vomiting a sort of scary thing. An unnatural thing, but I always felt better knowing that my mom was right next to me, preventing me from slamming my head straight into the bowl of the toilet. I was a serious puker. When I saw that Baxter was, literally, about to lose it, that memory kicked in. I knelt down next to him in the driveway, placed my left hand under his belly and my right hand on the top of his head. With one large bodily flex out came a good amount of what was, an hour ago, doggie dinner. And about a Toro bag full of grass.

"Ewwwww!" says Emmy.

"Nasty!" says Mommy.

"I'll get the hose," says Daddy.

And, as with people, as soon as Baxter was done vomiting you could see he felt much better. He finished up the experience with a nice, long pee and entered the house no worse for wear. My involvement ended with hosing a respectable pile of puke into the gutter and down the sewer, bringing the curtain down on yet another magnificent puking performance.

That evening, when we were laying in bed, Baxter's vomit once again came right back up.

"I think I know why Baxter ate that grass," Melissa mentions in between pages of the book she's reading.

I offer my own theory: "To make an already revolting job even more disgusting?"

I think he eats the grass to *make* himself throw up, you know? To make himself feel better."

I chew on Melissa's theory for a few seconds. "So, what you're saying is that Baxter is self-medicating?"

"I think he knows that eating the grass will make him puke. You saw it yourself."

She was right. He ate that grass, and a few minutes later I was hosing tummyache down the driveway. It seemed pretty obvious the two were connected.

"Maybe. I'm going to look it up tomorrow, see if I can find

something about it on the Internet. Think of all the people that take their dogs to the vet for an upset stomach, spend all that money, when all they had to do was let them trim an inch of fescue from the yard. He's a smart boy."

"He's a dog," Melissa says, "I wouldn't bestow a doctorate upon him just yet."

I kill the lights and go to sleep dreaming of a day when I can boast to the other dog owners in the neighborhood and proudly proclaim: "There he is, my Dachshund the gastroenterologist."

❦ ❦ ❦

Well, what do you know?

Apparently, dogs will often eat grass when they have an upset stomach. The general consensus is that grass blades tickle their throat and stomach lining; this sensation, in turn, may cause the dog to vomit, especially if the grass is gulped down rather than chewed.

"So, he knew what he was doing," Melissa says.

"Guess so."

"That's impressive."

"Eh, not really."

"Are you serious?" Melissa asks.

"It's wired in. It's not like he read about it in *Good Health* magazine or something. He's just doing what wolves were doing twenty thousand years ago. It's cool that he knows to do it, but it's not miraculous."

"You're right," Melissa says. "You know what's miraculous?"

"What's that?" I ask.

"Your ability to look at anything and everything in a negative light."

"How is that being negative? It's being realistic, and why are you so upset about it?"

"I'm not upset. It's that you can't even be a little impressed with the fact that Baxter knows how to make himself feel better!"

"Okay, I'm a little impressed," I offer. "Better?"

"You're such a pain."

"Maybe you should eat some grass and make that pain go away," I suggest.

"I've got a better idea," Melissa says. "Why don't you feed the dogs and I'll start dinner?"

"Deal!"

As I'm scooping the kibble and dropping some into each of their bowls, I realize just how stupid the conversation that Melissa and I just had was. Why was I so reluctant to admit that it was indeed a very cool thing that Baxter did? While I was playing with my laptop on the sofa, waiting for Melissa to finish dinner, I figured out why: I was envious.

I, too, wanted to feel better.

It was about ten years ago when I first uttered the word "depressed" to a medical professional. That wasn't easy for two reasons. The first is that I don't really like going to doctors to begin with. Given what I went through with my parents, the mere thought of going to a doctor or, God forbid, a hospital immediately sets my blood pressure rising. Which poses a problem for a hypochondriac. Yes, I'm the kind of person for which every headache isn't a headache at all, but rather a long-dormant malignant tumor getting ready to finally burst through my cranial cavity. The second reason it wasn't easy to tell a doctor that I thought I was depressed was because of my reluctance to tell anyone anything even remotely personal about myself. It would be admitting a weakness. I've always prided myself on being able to cope with any issue life could throw at me. Look at what I went through with my parents. When my dad collapsed I was the only one there. Literally! My mom and brothers were in New York, while my dad and I were living in California, attempting to sell the business that first brought us out there to begin with. I was the one the doctors spoke to. I was the one who had to hear that they didn't think my dad would make it through the night, and that I should call my mother and tell her to get out here as soon as she could. Me. I dealt with that.

But I handled it. I didn't lose my head. I didn't fall apart. I kept it together and did what had to be done. Which was why I was so reluctant to talk to a doctor about being depressed. Depressed. It barely sounded like something to even get worked up about. Cancer. Heart attack. Coma. Weighted words, worthy of intensive medical intervention. Depressed? Take a shower, get out of the house, and sack up, man! People get depressed when their favorite sports team loses. They get a little depressed when they don't get that long-promised raise. But that's not even depression, really; it's just a quick bout of disappointment.

But I knew what I was feeling wasn't just disappointment. Disappointment doesn't pin you down in your bed. It doesn't make the thought of eating any kind of food a meaningless, repulsive act. Disappointment doesn't make you crave darkened rooms or incite you to cry over absolutely nothing. With disappointment you curse a bit, shrug your shoulders, and move on; with depression you are silent, unable to move, and wholly terrified.

"So, are you happy yet?" my brother Steven asked me, two days after I started taking Prozac.

"Sure am! In fact, next week my doctor's going to up my dosage to giddy!"

Steven's assumption would have been funny if it weren't for the fact that I knew he was serious. There's a common misconception that Prozac is magic. That after taking your very first dose, you immediately see rainbows and unicorns. Quite frankly, I don't want to take any medication that offers such a result.

"Isn't it supposed to make you happy?" Steven asks me.

"Dude, I got the pills from Walgreens, not Merlin. It takes time for the medicine to go to work, and when it does it's not like I'm going to be balls-to-the-wall happy. I'm not even sure you'll be able to notice a difference."

"Then how will you know if it's working?" he asks me.

Hmmm. Good question.

"I'm not sure. I imagine I'll feel a difference in myself, in the way I look at things," I answer, not quite convincing myself.

"How do you see things now?"

"Shitty."

"So, if things start looking less shitty then you'll know it's working—right?"

"Yep. Maybe."

And that's the half-assed measure of effectiveness I went with in my relationship with Prozac. The funny thing is, it worked. A few weeks after starting to take the pill I began to feel a bit better. Maybe *better* is not the right word. *Less serious* might be a better way of putting it. I didn't constantly perceive everything as doom and gloom. It didn't erase any of my problems or diminish the challenges that life put in front of me. It simply made me view those challenges as simply that: challenges. Things that, while probably inconvenient and potentially painful, were surmountable. It wasn't like I felt my life went from zero to ten. It was that I stopped worrying about putting a number to my life at all. It was as if I were disconnecting all these extension cords I had been using to power all these worries that had been with me during the previous few months when my marriage to my first wife, Sharon, was disintegrating. As the number of wires reduced, so, too, did the worries.

Again, there was no *happy* involved. It was, as Steven had prophesied, a matter of things just becoming less shitty. And I'm here to tell you, don't underestimate the power of "less shitty."

As the years progressed, I started taking more medications for a variety of ailments. Before I knew it I had the medicine cabinet of a seventy-five-year-old woman. Taking a lot of medications, while beneficial to your health, can sometimes get a little psychologically overwhelming. It wasn't long before I was looking for a way to whittle down the number of those little amber-colored bottles. And there was never any question in my mind which one I wanted to toss: the happy pills.

I'm still taking them.

Turns out, reducing life's shittiness quotient isn't something you kick. It's a constant war you wage. I'm cool with it. But I'm still envious of Baxter. Not because I couldn't make myself throw up if I really wanted to. A finger or a bottle of ipecac would certainly do the trick, if need be. And, lord knows, I have a wealth of pills and capsules at my disposal for whatever physically ails me. I think I'm envious of Baxter because his solution is so simple. So natural. Shoot, it's literally right outside the door. I guess I wished there was something natural, something right outside *my* door that would work some magic that wasn't measured in milligrams. Imagine my surprise when I found out there was.

"You should try it."

"Babe, it's not my thing," I respond.

"You do it *every day*. How is it not your thing?"

"I do it to move, I don't do it to, you know, *move*!"

"I'm telling you, just try it. You'll see."

"I'm only going around the block."

"I bet you you'll want to go around the block more than once. Bet?"

"You're going to lose that bet."

"That's my problem."

"What are we betting?"

"If you go around the block more than once, and I *will* be watching, then you tell me I was right."

As I start walking down the driveway I yell without looking back, "Don't you get tired of making the same bet?"

"Surprisingly, no. Get moving!"

It gets exhausting being wrong.

I started walking.

And, as Melissa correctly predicted, I went around the block more than once. And I didn't hate it. I didn't love it, but it wasn't the worst feeling in the world. While I certainly wasn't breaking any speed records, I felt a surge of satisfaction as I blew past a couple of new mothers wheeling their pride-and-joys in their strollers. Hey, I'll take satisfaction wherever I can find it. I kept it up. Eventually, I moved up to the big league: a local park. There I walked up and down the hills and valleys of a blacktop path that wound through stands of pine and oak. Accompanied by a heavy metal soundtrack, I enjoyed walking for an hour of uninterrupted me time. Sure, the walking would end up helping me shed some weight which, in turn, would help lower my blood pressure. But, I think the greatest benefit of the walking was that it gave me a chance to unplug from the world. An hour-long respite from whatever was burdening my mind at that time, which could be anything and everything. For the longest time I looked at those people who would be power walking beside the road in all kinds of weather. "Nut jobs," I'd mumble, as I drove past them. Now I acknowledge my fellow nut jobs as we pass each other in the park, and I realize that if you can find something, anything, to make yourself better, no matter how silly it looks or ridiculous it sounds, do it. Like, I don't know, maybe eating grass?

I am still on Prozac—well, technically Fluoxetine, which is the generic version of Prozac. No sense being depressed *and* broke, right? But, more important, I'm still walking. And, it's still helping. The problems still arise, the challenges still block my way, but they don't quite seem as daunting as they once did. The mountains aren't quite as unclimbable. Who knows? Maybe it's just that I'm not as scared of everything as I once was. Or merely that life just doesn't seem as shitty. I don't really care what the reason is. I just know that I feel better. And, you'll be happy to know, so does Baxter.

He still occasionally gets an upset stomach. That'll happen when you pair the appetite of an elephant with the judgment of a tick. But a couple of laps around the yard, a bushel of grass blades and a handful of heaves later, and all is well. Well, maybe not well. Better! And better, I'm here to tell you, isn't so bad.

Dachshund Life Lesson #18

Heel thyself.

19

Running with the Big Dog (Singular)

They're not really the Odd Couple.

And I wouldn't classify them as friends.

I'm not really sure how to describe Baxter and Molly's relationship.

I guess I would say that they just always seem to be around each other. Which surprised all of us.

When we decided to have Molly join our family, we were immediately concerned as to how Baxter would react to the addition. He was fine when Maya joined the clan, mainly because Maya is a very low-key dog and because, in that amazing, unspoken way that dogs communicate with each other, Maya made it clear to Baxter right from day one not to mess with her. He has taken her at her word ever since.

We thought this time might be different: after all, two dogs are two dogs; three dogs is a pack. Plus, Molly was another girl. Would Baxter not like that? Would he start acting out in strange ways in order to make his displeasure known? Would he get physical with Molly? Baxter is three times her size and, with one ill-timed jump, could pretty much squash her. We were about to find out.

Turns out, we needn't have worried.

≈ ≈ ≈

Molly entered our home with little fanfare, a quiet confidence, and a wagging tail. She was a happy, refreshing, easy addition to our family. Of course, that's after you discount the fact that she immediately, and permanently, made Baxter her bitch.

Not in an overt, petrified, sleep-with-one-eye-open way. It was a lot subtler than that, with lots of physical posturing and eye contact. From the very first time we fed all three dogs together it was clear that Baxter would defer to Molly. First Maya knocked Baxter down a peg when she joined the family, and now he was scared shitless by a dog that looked like she ran on three AAA batteries. He stood there watching Molly walk confidently up to the big food bowl—Baxter's food bowl—and start chowing down on his food. He took half a step toward the bowl, and Molly immediately glanced one little eye his way. It was quick, but that was all that had to be said.

You may be wondering how Maya reacted to the addition of Molly to the crew. Fine. No problems. But that's Maya. She has seen things and experienced a lot of stuff that, I think, have mellowed her to the point of simply not caring about a lot of typical dog business. That, and the fact that Maya puts out an unmistakable don't-fuck-with-me vibe. She hardly ever growls at either of the dogs, and she never gets physical. There is just—I guess you'd call it an understanding between the three of them—that Maya is the Mac Daddy Dachshund. There is a scene in *Goodfellas* when Paulie, the big boss, first appears on-screen, and the voiceover says: "Paulie might have moved slow…but it was only because Paulie didn't have to move for anybody." It's kind of like that with Maya. And she does have a thing for Italian sausage.

But, with Baxter and Molly it's just different. And hysterical. It amuses us no end when Molly steals one of Baxter's rawhide bones and Baxter attempts to get it back. And, by getting it back, I mean that he sits there staring at Molly while whimpering like a bullied child. He'll then glance over at me, hoping that Daddy will intervene and right this terrible wrong. No chance. I'm a big believer in letting the dogs handle their own dog issues, and as I said, it never gets old watching this melodrama.

Sometimes, Baxter will attempt to squeeze himself in between Maya and Molly when they're laying on the couch or on their blue pillow. When he does, he'll sometimes accidentally step on Molly, or, he'll get just a bit too close for Molly's comfort. It's at those rare moments when I'm truly amazed at how such big, sinister sounds can come out of an animal that, in dim light, resembles a stuffed dog more than an actual dog. When she wants to, Molly can bring the scary shit with the best of them. And if his quick exit is any indication, Baxter finds it scary, too.

And yet, for all of Molly's bossiness with Baxter, she is his shadow.

Dog relationships fascinate me because they're anything but simple. Dachshund interpersonal dynamics are always on full display, constantly correcting and contradicting my beliefs that up until a month, or even a day ago, I firmly believed in. Baxter and Molly are a prime example. Take, for instance, pill time.

In addition to back problems, one of the illnesses common to Dachshunds is epilepsy. When Baxter was about two, he had his first seizure. While the type and duration of seizure that he had was pretty mild as seizures go, it was still very upsetting to witness. Fortunately, the vet said that medication could help control the frequency of his seizures. And, since that day, Baxter has been on antiseizure meds. Every morning and evening Baxter is given a little white pill wrapped up in a small piece of American cheese. And every morning and evening Molly tags along for moral support, especially when she discovered that Baxter's treatment involved the consumption of dairy products. In fact, it's gotten to the point where, when Melissa or myself yells to Baxter, "Pill time," it's *Molly* that arrives first in the kitchen. Doorbells also provide another opportunity for the Baxter-and-Molly dynamic to play out.

If there's one thing in life that I am sure of, it's that nobody is ever going to break into our house at night without us knowing it. All of the dogs are übervigilant when it comes to noises, especially outside noises. If a car pulls in the driveway, a siren sounds, or a dog is barking half a mile away, I'm going to know about it. Which is good. It's like possessing three relatively inexpensive, high-quality security systems. The downside being that you can't turn this particular security system off. Ever. That means that even the most minute of sounds gets the five-alarm treatment. And this alarm system has no respect for whether or not the disturbance is occurring during the day or night. It's gotten to the point where even ordering Chinese takeout requires a delivery strategy.

We're pretty sure that Maya recognizes the Chinese take-out menu, so, we've had to resort to placing the menu inside of a magazine or something, in order to conceal it from her eagle eyes. If she catches even a glimpse of a yin-yang symbol, we're in for thirty to forty-five minutes of high-pitched barking.

Then there is Baxter and Molly.

While Maya will bark like mad when the delivery guy shows up, she will never go down the stairs and actually head toward the front door. The same can't be said for Baxter or Molly. Like two cops on the beat, they are the ones who will run down the stairs and go right to the door. So, here is what Melissa and I do: I carefully position myself on the sofa so I can see the headlights of the delivery guy's car when he pulls into the driveway. When it arrives I can't actually say the words, "He's here." All of the dogs are familiar with that phrase, so we usually come up with a code word to be used only once, which will alert Melissa to the arrival of the food. And, this is the most important part: I can't say it with any kind of emotion or emphasis. I must speak it in a quiet, very matter-of-fact tone. The slightest hint of intonation or emotion will set them racing to the door.

Lights appear in the driveway.

Game time.

"Hon?" I say to Melissa with the emotion of Hal from *2001: A Space Odyssey.*

"Yes?" she questions sotto voce.

"The flower has bloomed. I repeat: the flower has bloomed."

With the practiced precision of Navy Seals, Melissa smoothly, yet quickly, grabs Baxter and proceeds to hold him in a firm grip, thereby immediately immobilizing him. At this point, Maya knows what's going on and begins her sonic serenade, which will not end until the car has left the driveway and the steamed dumplings have made their appearance. The only one left to deal with is Molly, which, truth be told, isn't much of a deal. A carefully placed foot is enough to keep her from running out the front door while I hastily scribble my name on the receipt and apologize to the delivery guy for all of the barking.

After the guy leaves I give the all clear signal, thereby releasing Baxter from Melissa's kung fu death grip, which is what's required to restrain twenty-five pounds of relentlessly squirming muscle. At that moment, Molly runs over to Baxter where, I guess, she debriefs her partner on the threat that is now gone and, more important, that the General Tso's chicken has arrived. I've often wished that we didn't like Chinese food as much as we do. But nothing gets past my dogs without them knowing. Including fortune cookies.

However, I think the most telling example of Baxter and Molly's unique relationship occurs when they're separated. Sometimes we'll opt to take Baxter or Molly to the vet or to the groomers individually. While this makes it a lot easier on us, neither Baxter nor Molly seem to like it. As we're backing out of the driveway with Baxter in the backseat with Emmy, we can all hear Molly inside the house voicing her displeasure. What makes this display so unique? Molly doesn't do it when we take Maya away from her, only Baxter. And Baxter, while not as vocal as Molly, always seems to be excited and relieved when Molly returns home from a visit to the vet. He rushes out of the garage and immediately begins to lick and sniff Molly's muzzle, while she is doing the same to him, as if they're noses will confirm what their eyes are seeing.

One minute they're getting along, and then we're hearing low growls and seeing raised hackles. They share like twins, and then it's every Dachshund for his or her own self. They are at peace, and then they're at war. I guess I have to finally admit what, for a long time, I've always suspected but was hesitant to voice, because we're talking about dogs here: Baxter and Molly are, much to my surprise, friends. At least, I *think* that's what friendship looks like.

My memory isn't exactly what it used to be.

❦ ❦ ❦

I had three best friends growing up. I've never been real clear on the criteria as to what exactly constitutes a best friend, but since I spent most of my time from the ages of thirteen to seventeen in the company of these three friends, I'll go ahead and apply the label to all three.

We met when I started sixth grade. As with many friendships, I can't really recall exactly how they began. But, knowing myself as I do, I can assume that it wasn't me who made the first move. I seem to remember all three as being the outgoing types. All were into sports. As time progressed we spent lots of time at each other's houses, our mothers taking turns feeding the other three with great regularity. We hung out after school, we were together on weekends, and we shared many summer nights drinking Boone's Farm Apple Wine on a short bridge that spanned a body of water that was simply and always referred to as "the Creek." Hmm. Funny how something as benign and unforgettable as a sad excuse of a creek plays such a large role in the memories of my youth, but there it is, winding and bending like a touchstone that I use to find my way back to those memories.

The four of us experienced our teenage years together, the good, the bad, and the pimply. We discovered the complicated dynamics of boy/girl relationships. We joined sports teams together. We each took celebratory first drives together after we received our driver's licenses. We went through a long period where we spent many Saturday nights at a local teenage disco, where, if you had a dollar to your name, you could indulge in a plastic cup filled with piña colada mix, sans the alcohol. This was the same time period where such names as Jordache, Sergio Valente, and Calvin Klein made nightly appearances on the asses of the girls and boys from the towns along Long Island's south shore. At the time it was the height of style and cool; in hindsight it was a deeply regrettable fashion faux pas. But for the most part, I remember it as a pretty wonderful time.

But the passage of time and changes in circumstance wreak havoc on friendships, no matter the decade or style trends. In the latter part of high school I somehow got involved in the drama club, which was, at least for me, a life-altering decision. It literally impacted what I did with the rest of my life and what I'm doing at this very moment: writing. However, drama club wasn't my only extracurricular activity. I was also on the football and baseball teams. As far as many of my teammates were concerned, I might as well have put on a tutu and proclaimed my gayness from the top bench of the bleachers. The term "drama fag" was used quite a bit. At the time I laughed about it, but it really bothered me. Mainly because I wasn't gay. But second, because the most vocal of my critics were the three guys in the world who were supposedly my best friends. I realize now that it was at that point that I started drifting apart from my best friends. I didn't go out for either football or baseball again. I started spending more of my time involved with the various drama club productions and my fellow thespians (they had a lot of fun with that one, too). But, the final nail in my friendship coffin with my friends was a sixteen-year-old brunette with piercing green eyes named Carole.

I think first girlfriends always hold a special place in a guy's heart. Probably, by virtue of the fact that they were the first ones to say yes. But Carole, aside from answering in the affirmative, also holds a distinction that no other woman in my life, not even my Melissa holds: Carole knew my parents. Even though I haven't seen Carole in almost thirty years, she still holds a special place in my heart because of that fact. When Carole entered the picture, my friendships faded quickly to black.

But that's not uncommon. Life is littered with stories of girlfriends or boyfriends breaking up long-lasting friendships. And Carole was a biggie—the first ones always are. In other words, it wasn't long before I was spending all of my waking hours with her and none with the three guys who, up until just a short while ago, were my constant companions. But, time and circumstance is an equal opportunity destroyer.

A move to California, shortly after I graduated high school, tore my relationship with Carole apart. So, there I was, three thousand miles away from the girl I loved, with zero friends and no clue as to what I was going to do with my life. Clearly, things had to get better. And, they did, but not before they got worse. Much worse.

＊ ＊ ＊

The death of my father is something that I will always carry with me. While my mom's death was equally terrible and in many ways worse, because of its long, painful duration, my dad's death is a wound that even thirty-one years later feels raw to the touch. I think it's because I was so alone at the time. Even today, when I think about how alone I was out there when my dad first fell ill, it leaves my stomach in knots.

My mom's illness was brutal, her demise all but ensured. I felt an exquisite kind of weakness, a sense of utter uselessness, as I watched my mother slowly fade from my life. Every failed treatment a reminder of what was coming; every day a step closer to being motherless. But at that point I was engaged to my first wife, and I had my brothers and other relatives to at least help bear the burden of watching a close relative waste away right in front of you. With my dad there was only me.

People often joke that a real friend is the one who, with no advance notice, will gladly get in his or her car and pick you up at the airport. I'm here to tell you that there is no moment when friends become realer, and more valued, then when you bury a parent. At least, I think that's the case. I couldn't say, because when I buried mine, my onetime best friends were nowhere to be seen.

∗ ∗ ∗

I am amazed when people tell me that they still hang out with their friends from high school. The first thought that usually pops into my head is *How sad. How sad that you have to cling to the memories of high school instead of embracing your life today.* Close behind that first thought is this second thought: *That's just wonderful.*

I've lived thirty years without the chance to share those years with the three people who were there at the beginning. I've never had the opportunity to sit down and laugh about those nights, when we worried about whether or not we had that precious extra dollar to buy that special girl that virgin piña colada. Part of what makes the memories of youth so sweet is the ability to look back on those memories with the very people who helped make them memories in the first place. I never had that chance. And that has made those memories much less palatable. The older I get the more sour they become.

≈ ≈ ≈

Melissa and I talk a lot about the fact that neither of us really has a circle of friends. At this very moment, if I had to call someone with either good or bad news, I would have nobody to call other than my brother Steven. I have nobody whom I would willingly categorize as a friend. I *know* many people. There are lots of folks I would call acquaintances, and many of them are perfectly nice people and I am perfectly nice to them. But if I need a ride home from the airport, I'm cabbing it. I'm not sad about this. I'm a big-time introvert, and I'm very comfortable with my own company. And, of course, Melissa truly is my best friend. But in terms of people who aren't related to me, there is no one. That's fine, but it hasn't stopped me from wondering...

...if all of those *drama fag*s raining down upon me left deeper marks than I thought they did. I wonder if three empty spots at my parents' gravesites hardened me. I look back at sixth grade and wonder if any of it mattered in the end.

And then I wonder if any of it was my fault.

Sure, I've had to endure some tragedies in my life. So? At one time or another, everyone does. I never went out of my way to stay in touch with my friends from those long ago days. As the years passed I never reached out to rekindle something that time smothered to something less then cold ashes. While I hate to admit it, I suppose I'm just as guilty as they are. I have no friends because I choose not to have friends. And now I'm afraid it's too late. I feel like I am too fully formed. Far too set in my ways. My patience is, as we all know at this point, questionable. How does one who is nearing fifty go out and make friends? I wouldn't even know where to start. So the friend ship has sailed. But don't feel bad for me. I'm really good with all of it. Seriously. It's just that, well, sometimes I still wonder...

≈ ≈ ≈

Friendships are neither easy to form nor maintain. One look at Baxter and Molly tells me that it's not always rawhide and rainbows. And sure, when I see them treating each other sweetly, I do wonder if I should maybe try harder, or at least keep myself open to the thought of making some friends. I suppose I still am. Besides, it's not long before I realize that the friends I want and, more important, the friends I need are already in my life. At this moment, one of them is barking in anticipation of some Szechuan beef. One is being physically restrained by my very best friend in the world. And another is taking in all of the details, so she can report back to her partner in crime.

Dachshund Life Lesson #19

*All you need are one
or two good friends.
Any species will do.*

CHAPTER 20

All Creatures Great and Still Very Much Moving

I have grown accustomed to my dogs tasting, testing, and trying things with their mouths. They are dogs, after all, and a dog's primary way of investigating the world, outside of its nose, is with its mouth. Consequently, I've seen a great many things wedged firmly between canine molar and incisor: tree branches, paper plates, sponges, flower bulbs, socks, clothes dryer lint, wrapping paper, pencils, extension cords, dirty underwear, bubble wrap, eggshells, chewing gum, aluminum foil, straws, baseball caps, and used coffee filters, to name just a few. It's been so many years and so many items that at this point, it would take something really out of the ordinary to faze me.

"Daddy! Baxter's got a candle in his mouth," Emmy alerts me one day.

"Don't worry about it, baby," I yell from the living room, where I'm watching a football game.

"But, daddy, he's got a candle *in his mouth*!"

Sigh.

"Is it lit?"

A couple seconds of silence. "Uh, no."

"Then I'll be there on the next commercial."

As I said, I've pretty much seen it all, and all of it has hung, at one time or another, out of a Dachshund's mouth. In fact, I can think of only one instance where I was actually surprised by what one of the dogs had in its mouth, and I was surprised for two reasons. The first reason was because the dog was Maya.

By this point in the story you've probably formed a fairly accurate profile of Maya: namely, that she has some serious psychological baggage. You would be correct. She sure as hell does. You'd also be correct in saying that she's highly predictable, never really deviating from her typical daily routine. Again, well done. And that was why I was totally stunned when she did something so far out of the norm for her. Let me put it this way, if I knew what was *going* to happen ahead of time, I would have bet my money on Baxter being the culprit. But it wasn't Baxter. As with people, sometimes a dog will surprise you.

The second reason I was so surprised by what she had in her mouth was—hmmm—how do I explain this?

Okay, if you're a dog owner, you simply get used to seeing your dog have things in their mouths. It just comes with the territory. Many of those things are strange, a lot are gross, and many are just plain silly. But, they don't usually have something in their mouth to make a grown man scream. That would be me—the grown man who screamed. That's because of all of the words that can be used to describe what it is that's hanging from your dog's mouth, the very last word you want to pluck from the dictionary is this one: *flapping*.

Every so often we'll find a dead sparrow or robin in the backyard, a victim of a really bad snowstorm, a poorly judged landing, or a cat that's successfully channeled its inner lion. The dogs will usually sniff around it, but I'll shoo them away from the poor thing before they've had a chance to dredge themselves in Eau d' Birdy. And, of course, there are certain dogs bred specifically to spot and retrieve birds, so the sight of a dog with a bird in its mouth, while certainly unpleasant, wouldn't really freak me out. And let's face it: the particular breed of dog in *my* yard is only interested in a bird if it's been marinated in ginger dressing and is currently boasting a killer set of grill marks. Would a bird in the mouth be gross? Sure. Scream-inducing gross? Doubtful.

So by now you've probably used your basic knowledge of flora and fauna to whittle down the possible critters that Maya was holding in her mouth. Let's be honest—there aren't all that many things that flap. But since you weren't there and I was, I really want to try to convey to you what it was like when I saw what I saw, because to this day, the mere thought of it gives me a raging case of the willies. What kind of friend would I be if I didn't at least attempt to share that experience with you, my very favorite reader in the whole, entire world?

The focal point of our family room is a large, sliding glass door that looks out over a good portion of our backyard. I like this door, because when I'm sitting on the couch the door almost acts as a large picture frame, providing me with a big, unobstructed landscape view of the woods that back up to our house. I find it quite easy to simply sit there and stare and, as Baxter has made crystal clear to all of us, the art of staring is woefully underestimated. So, this large, lovely window affords me lots of opportunities to practice my art. Stop looking at me like that—we all need hobbies.

On occasion, I'll let the dogs out in the yard for a quick visit, so that big sliding glass door allows me to keep an eye on the dogs while still applying my ass firmly to the couch. Besides, I have a pretty solid handle on what each dog does when they're out back, so it's not like I have to watch each of them every single second.

There is a corner of the leather sofa in our family room that, through an incredible amount of research and personal sacrifice, I've been able to determine is one of the most comfortable, ass-friendly seats in our entire house. Not only does it afford me the best possible position in which to watch the big-screen television that dominates the room, it also allows me to keep a watchful eye on the dogs. But sometimes, due to the ridiculously comfortable nature of the couch, I lose focus and get too drawn in to whatever is on television, and I forget that there are three dogs outside in an unfenced yard, doing dog stuff.

On one such day, probably when there was a good football game on television, I lost total visual contact with the dogs. I remember it was a bright, sunny day. It might have been late summer or early fall. All I recall is that the dogs were outside, they weren't barking, and that was good enough for me.

At some point, out of my peripheral vision I saw a bit of black-and-tan just outside the glass slider, the very top of someone's head. That usually means that whoever that black-and-tan belonged to probably wanted to come back inside. I watched a few more seconds of the game before I began to slowly peel myself from the couch. As I did I was looking in the direction of whoever it was that was standing outside the door, and as I got up I saw more and more of the dog. As I finally stood completely up, I realized that it was Maya who was asking to be let in. I took one step toward the door. And then I stopped. The kind of stop that happens when your brain tells you something like *You need to stop right now!!!* At the same time when my brain was putting on the brakes, my eyes detected that Maya was holding something firmly in her mouth. My first natural assumption, given the fact that it was Maya, was that the object in her mouth was a piece of poop. However, as far as I knew, we didn't have any cattle grazing in our yard, and this thing in her mouth was quite a bit larger than the usual animal turds Maya retrieves. Another thing that also made me doubt that this was a piece of crap was that it was black. I mean, jet-black. My mind said *turd*, but my eyes told me that it just wasn't the case.

A bird! That's it! She's got a bird in her mouth. That's a relief, I thought to myself. But that relief didn't last long.

Where are the feathers?

If it was a bird in her mouth, there should have been some

feathers on the patio or the grass or something. I didn't see any feathers. It was at this point when my mind went to a very bad, dark place. Keep in mind that I was still standing in the middle of the family room staring at Maya. And Maya hadn't budged. She was standing at the base of the step outside, tail wagging, with this…thing lodged in her mouth. She looked happy. I did *not* look happy. And, even worse, an image began to form in my mind that was not going to make whatever was about to happen pleasant.

"Hon!" I yelled to Melissa, who was in the living room.

"Yeah?"

"Uh, can you come here for a sec? Maya has something in her mouth."

"So, take it out!"

"I need you to take a look at this."

I have no research or figures to back me up on this, but I'm fairly certain that nothing good has ever come after the words "I need you to take a look at this" have been spoken. I heard Melissa walking toward the family room, the urgency of her stride telling me that she already suspected something was amiss.

She arrived, stood next to me, and looked at Maya. "What the fuck is that?"

"I don't know. Maybe it's poop?" I wishfully proposed.

"Poop? Where are we, the Serengeti? Look at the size of that…thing!"

I knew she was right, but I really didn't want to let go of the poop argument, because the alternative was so much worse.

"It's some kind of bird," Melissa offered.

"What makes you think it's a bird?"

"Because you can see, if you move over a bit, that piece that's sort of sticking out a bit looks like a wing. You see that? And you know Maya, she loves dead things, and we have had dead birds in the yard before. That's definitely what it is, it's a bird."

My wife has a ridiculous track record of being right. Like a "You can bet money on it" kind of track record. And Maya does have a history with dead birds. But something told me that record was about to fall.

"Babe," I calmly said, "where are the feathers?"

The pause lasted awhile.

"Maya probably chewed them off, or, I don't know, plucked them or something."

"Then, where are they? I mean, wouldn't there be some on the patio, or the grass? I don't see a single feather anywhere."

An even longer pause.

Melissa and I looked at each other, both arriving at the same conclusion at the exact same time, but neither one of us was willing to voice the word. The B word.

Maya's tail seemed to be wagging faster. She really wanted in.

My wife slowly and carefully began to speak. "If that thing in Maya's mouth is what I think it might be, I am telling you right now, that I am going to be beyond freaked out. Seriously. She is not coming in, and I am not going out there."

"Hon," I said, "if it is what you think it is, and what *I* think it is, someone's going to have to go out there and convince

Maya to drop it. She might contract some kind of disease from that thing, who the hell knows. But we have to do something now!"

"Let me be clear," my wife reiterated, "I am *not* going out there. *You* are going out there. Matt, I am a few dry heaves from losing my breakfast. You are going out there and making her drop it."

My wife rarely calls me by my name, and when she does, it's never a sign of good things to come.

"Okay, go into the garage right now and get me the broom and a pair of those gardening gloves," I instructed her. Our eyes never left that black demon in Maya's mouth. Melissa pulled herself away from the room and headed to the garage. Trying to calm myself, and in a weak attempt to psych myself up for what I was about to do, I yelled to Melissa, now in the garage, "Hey! Babe? It could be worse, you know? At least the thing is dea—*OH MY GOD, OH MY GOD, OH MY GOD!!!!!*"

This is the part where I was screaming like a girl. About the only thing I had going for me now was that Melissa was screaming, too, as she ran back into the family room with the broom and the gloves.

"What is it? What is it?" she asked me, her eyes big and scared.

I whispered, trying to maintain whatever semblance of self-control I have left, "It's still alive. I just saw one of its wings flap!"

So we did the most logical thing at a moment like this. We both began yelling at Maya through the glass door.

239

"Maya! Drop it! Maya, *drop it*! Come on Maya, drop the bat! *Maya!!* Maya *please* baby, *drop it*!!!"

But that wasn't what Maya heard. Maya heard, "Good girl, Maya! Good girl. Who's a good girl? Who's a pretty, good girl?" If anything, she stood more erect, her ears perked up, and her tail began to move even faster, a happy metronome.

Different people react differently in stressful situations. Under stress I tend to get quiet in an attempt, I guess, to hear myself think. The next thing I knew I heard myself speak with the slow, deliberate pace one usually associates when one is attempting to dismantle a ticking bomb:

"Okay, hand me those gloves and the broom. You're going to open the slider enough for me to squeeze outside, when I do, quickly close it behind me. I am then going to lean the broom against the house, after which I will put on the gloves, then, I am going to pick up Maya and carry her to the grass. Once there, I'm going to get the broom and use it to try to sweep the bat out of Maya's mouth. Once I do, I'm going to use the broom to stun the bat. Then I'm going to pick it up with my glove and toss it over the back fence."

"You think that'll work?" Melissa asked me.

"Babe, I don't have a 'how to remove a bat from a dog's mouth' template to work from. Give me a fucking break! I'm trying to just hold it together. Work with me!"

Sometimes, things have an amazing way of working out. My half-assed plan actually worked. I donned the gloves and grabbed the broom, Melissa opened the sliders, I carried Maya to the grass, holding her at arm's length, I swept at and stunned the bat, said bat got tossed over the fence, I succeeded in keeping the food that was in my stomach in my stomach, Melissa threw out the broom and burned the gloves, and Maya went into the house and acted as if me sweeping a still-living bat from her mouth was just another day at the office.

To this day, Melissa and I think of that event and our skins collectively crawl. But, to Maya, it was probably another time when Daddy wouldn't let her eat something that she found outside. While Melissa and I were freaking out beyond any previous freak-outs on record, Maya stood there, posture high and tail wagging. In fact, she was probably looking at us through the sliding glass door and thinking to herself, *Is there something wrong with the glass door? Is it cracked? Smudged? That high-pitched screaming is really hurting my ears.*

After, what quickly became known as "the flying rat day," we dubbed Maya the queen of underreaction. What will it take to get a rise out of Maya? I shiver considering the possibilities, but rest assured we are well stocked on garbage bags, industrial-use gloves, an extralong broom, and enough Purell to service a fair-sized, regional medical center. But if Maya is the reigning queen of underreaction, then it's entirely possible that I might be the reigning king of *over*reaction. And it usually takes a helluva lot less than a still-breathing bat to set me off.

❧ ❧ ❧

"Don't answer it," I instruct Melissa as the phone continues to ring.

"What if it's something important?"

"What are the odds of that, seriously?"

"Well, I won't know unless I answer it."

"But, if you *don't* answer it, it *definitely* will be nothing important," I say with the kind of conviction that Einstein must have had when he unveiled his theory of relativity. Only my theory sounds like it's coming from a crazy person, which, of course, it is.

"Hello," Melissa pleasantly speaks into the receiver, while looking at me as if I just farted in her face.

So much for relativity.

"Nope, you have the wrong number. It's okay, bye."

She places the phone back in its cradle and fixes me with a look. "You know, it's just a phone call. There's no reason to assume it's going to be bad news or someone you don't want to speak to, or some bell of doom tolling."

"Maybe you're right. Maybe I need to reassess my phone policy," I offer.

"You *think?* Let's start with the fact that you even *have* a phone policy! Get over it, babe."

As I was saying, I might have a bit of an overreaction problem. Not sure why. And this isn't about me being a pessimistic person. This is something entirely different. I mean; *I have a phone policy.* What's next? A mail-opening protocol? A showering game plan? The very fact that I'm sitting here thinking about what I just wrote and *not* considering them totally out of the realm of possibility and normalcy tells me—and you—all I need to know. I might be ready for a little intervention. But that's just a small example of my tendency to overreact.

Going to the movies.

I don't go often for the simple reason that I hardly ever enjoy the experience. And yes, before you ask me if I have some kind of movie thing, *yes*, I do have a movie thing. Although, I don't really think of it as a movie *thing*, thank you very much. It's just good, movie-viewing sense.

We always arrive long before the movie is to begin, at least forty-five minutes. This is sort of along the lines of my airport plan. The thought of entering an already darkened theater that is already playing previews and muttering "Excuse me, excuse me" as I sidle my way toward a seat seems ridiculous to me, and completely unnecessary. I never get popcorn or drinks because I've never felt the need for a Hefty bag's worth of popcorn or a container of soda measured in liters. But the most critical movie-viewing decision has to do with seating. I never, ever sit in the middle section of the theater; I always sit on the sides.

Everyone knows that the best place to view a movie is in the middle, allowing you to see the screen straight on and get the full effect of the cinematography. And because everyone knows this, the middle section seats are the first seats to be taken. Selecting a seat in the middle section of the theater is like slathering yourself in honey and then having someone release a swarm of bees. It's never long before a family of seven, with four kids under the age of ten, make their way to the row directly in front of me, where the mother will then engage in distributing candy, popcorn, and drinks that she opted to purchase, rather than, say, paying that month's rent. Soon, other worker bees are taking seats behind me and, God help me, *next to me*, which then leads to an unavoidable battle for the armrest.

There is nothing more annoying than having an unspoken, brutal armrest battle. I never quite know the rules of engagement for something like this. How far should I go to defend that which is mine? Hey! Did I just detect a discernible shove from the specimen next to me? Do I shove back, or, do I just apply steady pressure until I banish her bastard elbow from the battlefield? I do neither. I choose to fight another day. In other words, I sit on the side.

Sure, those side seats are the redheaded stepchildren of the movie theater experience, but it's that very reason that it appeals to me. By placing myself there, I'm playing the odds that the moviegoing public will move toward the middle section, already deep into their jumbo packs of Twizzlers.

It's five minutes before the previews start, and we're the only ones on the side. Things are looking good. The lights start to dim. The curtain widens. I lean back in my chair, give Melissa a smile, knowing she's just as happy as me about our self-banishment from the middle section, and get ready to enjoy—*ah shit!*

Three shadows noisily skulk into the row *right in front of us*. There are plenty of empty rows on the side section. There is no logical reason as to why they've chosen the row in front of us. And without fail, it is always the woman with the Texas-teased hair that sits in front of Emmy. It's at this moment that

Melissa glances over at me, pantomimes her *What the fuck* look of annoyance, and points at the empty rows behind us. We're on the move.

We quickly, and quietly, move back three rows, which now affords us an unobstructed view. For exactly fifteen seconds. I'm not going to bore you with what happens next, because you know what happens next. Every empty row quickly becomes a full row with lots and lots of hungry, munching theatergoers. Which is why I'm not a theatergoer but rather a theater avoider. And, for the sake of our little discussion here, one might say, a theater overreactor.

Melissa begins the postmovie conversation in the car on the way home. "Babe. What can I tell you, it's a movie. There are going to be people at the movie. There are going to be people who eat popcorn at the movie. I'm not a fan of people sitting in front of us; that's why we moved seats. The rest of it I can't control. Did you at least *like* the movie?"

"Oh, was there a movie playing? I couldn't tell with all of the rustling of popcorn bags and slurping of sodas and coughing and sneezing, and—"

"How can you not know, Daddy?" Emmy interrupts from the backseat.

"Because, baby, I was too focused on those idiots behind us, who apparently felt that the best place to have an in-depth discussion about their girlfriend who's dating the guy who's afraid to make a commitment would be a packed movie theater where foolish people like us thought, might make for a great place to watch, oh, I don't know, a *movie*?"

"You really shouldn't go to movies anymore, seriously," Melissa declares.

"None of us should! It's just awful!"

At that moment Melissa's cell phone rings. She fumbles for it in her pocketbook.

"You're going to answer that?" I inquire.

"Why wouldn't I?"

And round and round we go.

Melissa, for whatever reason, thinks there's something to astrology. And, over the years I've come to know by rote the traits and tendencies of a Pisces, which is my birth sign. Supposedly, Pisces are sensitive, loving, highly creative, quiet, intelligent, loyal individuals who tend to avoid confrontation and opt for more subdued, solitary interests than other signs. And, they hate going to movies. I plan on submitting that last nugget to whoever is in charge of publishing horoscopes. But as much as I hate to admit it, I think there is something to the whole astrological sign thing. Especially that bit about being sensitive.

Turns out that, like an apple, I bruise easily. I never really thought of myself as that kind of person, the kind who not only suffers the slings and arrows of outrageous fortune but also gets great, big, lasting black-and-blues from them. Then again, as you're growing up you just don't take the time or have the inclination to look at yourself in the mirror and try to figure out what kind of person you are. If I did that when I was thirteen or fourteen, the answer would have been a pimply, braces-wearing, painfully shy, awkward-around-girls kind of person. The pimples and braces eventually went away; the rest appear to be in it for the long haul.

Besides, all you ever hear as a child is that the world is a big, tough place and you need to be an equally tough person to counter everything that the world will throw at you. At least in that regard, my parents were sure as hell right. But whatever sensitivity I might have had as a child wasn't really noticed by my father. Don't get me wrong: my dad wasn't exactly the Great Santini, but he also didn't spend any of his spare time reciting Emily Dickenson. I just think he didn't know how to deal with a kid who was more on the sensitive side, and by *deal with*, I mean "talk to." He just didn't really know how to come at me. My mom, on the other hand, was a different story.

My mom and I were close. "Mama's boy" probably fits me. It was only when I was an adult, and especially after she died, that I admitted something to myself that I think I knew all along but was reluctant to admit, especially when I was a teenager: My mom knew me. Really knew me, in a way that my dad never did. Listen, I loved my dad a lot, and I know he loved me. It's just that my mom knew me on a whole other level. Not that I have any monumental memories or moments that I could point to and say, "See, right there, she gets me." As with most mothers and sons, it was the little things that made me realize that I was fine the way that I was. I wished I realized that when I was young and, more important, when she was still alive—but, hey, I realize it now, and that still counts. Now that I think about it, though, there was this one time that I can clearly recall how, in an instant, my mom knew what her shy, overly sensitive son needed.

🦴 🦴 🦴

About a year after my dad died, I met a girl. Her name was Lynne. We met at a Long Island nightclub called Uncle Sam's. It might have been during the holidays because she was home from school. To say that I fell hard for Lynne is an understatement of incalculable proportions. She became my hobby, my job, and my obsession. Seriously, it might have been bordering on something unhealthy, but what did I care? I was madly in love with her. I would drive from Valley Stream, on the south shore of Long Island, all the way up to Oyster Bay, on the north shore, practically every day. Or she would drive to me. Whatever money I was earning working as an usher in a local movie theater went toward gas for my Dodge Dart. Every dollar went toward my Lynne addiction. In between spending every waking hour with each other, and using our bodies as amusement parks, we made plans. We explored the hidden coves and wooded roads of the north shore. She showed me where Billy Joel used to live before he had to move because too many kids would park outside his gated driveway and blast his songs on their car stereos. She even showed me his signature in her yearbook, obtained when Lynne and some classmates saw him one day in downtown Oyster Bay. I thought that was cool. I thought *everything* Lynne did and said was cool. I spent time with her family; she adored my mom. She was beautiful, and she was crazy smart.

She was attending SUNY Albany, majoring in computers and banging out As like they were slow-pitch softballs. School was important to her parents, and it was important to her. I knew that right from the beginning. I just didn't know that her desire to make something of herself would ultimately lead to our ending.

I didn't want her to go back to Albany in the fall. I spent a good part of our summer together trying to convince her to transfer to a school back on Long Island so we could be together. She had one year before she graduated. She told me she would continue to write me letters and we would talk on the phone a couple of times a week, just like we did the previous semester. That wasn't good enough for me. I hounded her about it. But she simply couldn't do it. She would finish school, graduate, come back to me, and we would focus on us. I told her that if she insisted on going back to Albany then she wouldn't ever see me again. The passage of time, and the weakening of memory, often makes it hard to clearly recall decisions that you made in the past, to try to determine whether certain decisions were wrong or right, meaningless or consequential. Even after thirty years, I can look back at that one decision and know that it was completely, terribly, and regretfully wrong. I overreacted.

We broke up. I was a fool. And I was devastated.

I went home and told my mother about it. She knew how much Lynne meant to me—and she truthfully loved Lynne—but she did her motherly duties, reciting the standard responses when your firstborn's heart is broken: "You're going to be just fine. There are lots of girls out there who will be lucky to have you for a boyfriend." I had failed to mention to my mom that it was I who was responsible for the breakup. That it was me, blinded by love, who failed to see the perfect logic in waiting. Eventually, I told her. And, she said all of the same things that Lynne had said to me during the last conversation in her driveway. I knew my mom was right, as I knew Lynne was right. But, I also knew it was too late. The way I reacted with white-hot fury when Lynne told me that she wasn't going to transfer to a local school sealed my fate. Her parents thought I was insane. And for the next couple of weeks, as I flagellated myself with a whip made of memories, I thought I was, too.

I couldn't eat. I moped. I saw no interest in seeing any-one or doing anything. I went through the motions of my job at the movie theater like a zombie. One night, right before I knew Lynne was planning on heading back to Albany, I made another bad decision. I drove, unannounced, to her house.

I sat in my car a few houses down from her house. Night had fallen. I sat there hoping to catch just a glimpse of her. I knew at the time that what I was doing was pathetic and sad. But, what did I care? That was pretty much how I felt.

I don't know how long I sat there, but at some point I noticed headlights in my rearview mirror. I slunk down in my seat a bit, not wanting to be noticed. As the car drew closer I realized that it wasn't her dad's car. I didn't know this car. The car drove past me, but then it pulled into Lynne's driveway, and before it even fully registered in my brain, I saw Lynne getting out of the passenger side of the car, and some guy get-ting out from behind the wheel.

He walked her up the front path to the front door. They spoke for a moment or two. She laughed at something he said, and then he slowly leaned in and gave her a kiss. It wasn't a long kiss. But it was enough evidence to make me realize that what I once had was gone.

After she went inside, and the car in the driveway pulled out and drove away. I started my car and, with headlights off, slowly drove past Lynne's house, pausing just a moment to watch the light in her room switch on. I drove away in shame and tears.

When I got home I went to my room which, mercifully, was empty. I was back to sharing a room with my brothers at that time, and they both were out. I flopped on the bed, my throat thick with emotion, my eyes hot from tears. I was facing the wall, so I didn't see my mom come into the room. She sat down next to me on the bed. I didn't turn to face her. She began to stroke my head. The tears began to flow once again. I buried my face in the pillow, not able to find the will to turn to my mom and tell her what I had done, and how irreparably broken I felt.

"Matthew, turn around."

Sniffling and wiping my eyes with the back of my hand, I flipped over and faced my mom.

"I know you're hurt. And there's nothing I can tell you right now to take that hurt away. I know you don't want to hear this, but over time that hurt will change."

"To what, Mom? *Everlasting pain?*" I threw back in her face, as I attempted to bury mine in the pillow once again.

She grabbed my shoulders. "Look at me! It will turn into

good memories. What you're feeling right now will change to the things you did with each other, the places you went together. You won't feel angry, or hurt, or stupid, or any of the feelings that you're having now. Matthew, you're going to find out that there are two ways your life can go, honey. There are the decisions you make on your own—and yes, sometimes you will make the wrong ones. And there are the decisions that life will make for you. It won't ask whether you're going to like it or not. If you're ready for it or not. Both hurt, but either way you're going to have to react to those kinds of decisions the same way."

"Which is...?"

"You go on. You just keep going on."

She started pushing my hair out of my sore eyes. A few seconds pass, mostly silent except for my sniffling.

"Am I going to be okay, Mom? Because right now, it doesn't feel like I will."

"Matty," my mom said with a slightly trembling lip, "we're *all* going to be okay."

For a moment, Lynne wasn't the loss we were speaking about.

Now my lips were trembling. "I really miss him."

"Me, too."

We sat there on my bed, hugging each other, our tears and sniffles comingled.

"Life really sucks sometimes, huh?" I asked my mother.

"It sure does. But I want you to know that there will always be a place where you'll be safe. That I can promise. Where there's no hurt, no rejection, no regrets, and no judgment. Where it doesn't matter *how* you react."

With my head resting on my mother's shoulder, and my tears finally ebbing, I asked, "Where's that?"

Pulling me closer, she kissed the top of my head and placed her wet cheek upon it. "You're leaning on it."

I closed my eyes and hugged the mother of a sensitive son.

≈ ≈ ≈

Thankfully, Maya's experience with the bat was a one-off deal. Since then, she's reverted back to picking up good old twigs, and bugs, and cat poop. Oh, happy days! As for my reaction when it happened, given the circumstances, I think I was well within the bounds of acceptable behavior. I guess that's the thing with reactions: they're totally dependent on the situation and, of course, the person experiencing that situation. A catastrophe to you may not seem like all that much of a big deal to me, and a live bat in a dog's mouth might not freak you out at all, when—well, I think you know where I stand on that.

I overreact. I know it and I accept it, mainly because I know that's just how I'm wired. Sometimes that will serve me well, and others, as history has proven, not so well. Thus far I think it's more or less balanced out, although I certainly don't see any matinees in my immediate future. But I really think I am going to make more of a concerted effort to be a little less reactionary. Just a bit. Try to be a little less sensitive to things that happen to me and with the things that people say to me.

Go against the old astrological assumptions. Try to count to ten, that whole thing.

I have no illusions. I know that it will be an uphill battle. It's not easy changing that original, internal wiring. But I'll give it a shot. And if I sometimes fail, so what? There are a lot worse things than the occasional overreaction, or being a little oversensitive, am I right?

Like a bat that never says die.

Dachshund Life Lesson #20

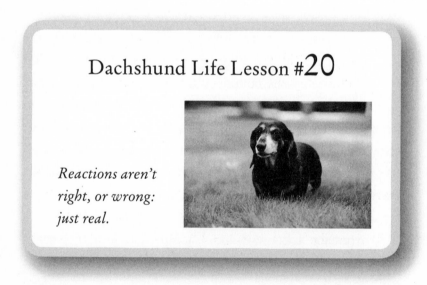

Reactions aren't right, or wrong: just real.

21

Dream Wiener

Dreams are often most profound when they seem the most crazy.

Sigmund Freud

It is easy for me to watch Molly dream and to believe that she is dreaming of running in a verdant, green meadow, or on a windswept beach with the scent of the ocean and all of its inhabitants assaulting her senses, or, in some alternate world where there are nothing but pieces of cheese and fire hydrants, drenched with the scent of dogs down through time. The reality is that I look at Molly dream, and I am utterly clueless as to what she might be dreaming about. I have my wishes, and I want them to be all of the things I mentioned above, because I wish her a world such as that. I wish that for all dogs and, with the exception of the fire hydrants, that wouldn't be all that bad of a gig for us humans, either.

She is, in a sense, my child, and what parent doesn't wish the very best for his or her child? But it's also frustrating, because like all people who own and love dogs, I want to know more than just what they dream about. I want to know what they're thinking. *How* they're thinking. I want to understand what they feel, because I think that to a large degree, I envy what they feel. I want to be *that* in the moment. I want to live for nothing more than the sake of living. I want to explain to them what they mean to me, what impact they're having on my life. I want them to know that I do not consider them just pets but true and real members of our family, valued with the same amount of respect and love that I have for the people in my family. But that's the rub with owning a dog, isn't it? What we want out of the relationship has to end there. We can't make them understand. We can go no further. That is the lasting barrier that separates us from dogs. And so, instead of knowing what they think and them knowing what we truly feel, we lavish them with love and attention and rawhide bones and scraps from our plates, as if all of that were a sufficient replacement for what we really want. It isn't, but it's all we've got.

So she lies there on the sofa, nose to tail, emitting a steady stream of high-pitched squeaks, eyes twitching, legs pumping, and all I can do is hope her dreams are the good kind. Sometimes I'll rest my hand lightly on her side, above her rising and falling ribs, just to let her know that I am there. To reassure her that in a world where everything isn't all cheese and fire hydrants, there is someone who, well, is just there. I don't want her to be scared, I don't want any of my dogs to be scared. But I *do* want them to dream.

I said it at the beginning of this book and, now that we've come to the end, I'll have you know that nothing has changed. I still think: Who am I to write a book? Where do I get off assuming that anyone anywhere would be even remotely interested in the story of a guy who thinks his Dachshunds are teaching him lessons about life? I'm more than a little dubious about the whole thing—*and I'm the guy with the three wieners*! So you may very well be sitting there posing the question that I've posed to myself at the beginning of each chapter: If you doubted throughout this whole project that anyone would care about what you have to say, why keep writing? Why put yourself through that kind of aggravation?

The easy answer, but not necessarily the simple answer, is that I don't know.

In my efforts to be clear, entertaining, funny, and honest, every page, sentence, and word has posed a challenge. Especially that honest part. It may be the best policy, but it sure isn't easy to put into twelve-point type for the world to read. And there have been instances when the time between writing sessions was getting longer and longer, while every time I sat down at the laptop, it was getting harder and harder to find a way to begin. I tend to think of writing as a journey (there's certainly nothing unique about that), and for me, that journey often felt as if I were constantly trying to get on the highway but was having difficulty finding a suitable on ramp. A place where I could merge with other writers who also have a story to tell. I'd be lying if I said I wasn't relieved to come to the end of this particular road trip. Dorothy Parker was quoted as saying, "I hate writing. I love having written." I think that about covers my feelings at this moment. While the traffic was horrendous, I'm awfully glad I got to where I was going.

I had this long-simmering dream of writing a book. And, regardless of whether or not these words ever see the light of day or the fluorescent lights of an Amazon distribution center or the bookstore shelves, I did what I set out to do. I sat down to write a book, and a book was written. It's done. And for that I am proud. But I think of Baxter, Maya, and Molly, and I wonder if what I have done for them is worthy of what they have done for me, because they have done much. I worry that I haven't thoroughly conveyed what they mean to me. I'm concerned that their lessons will come off as nothing more than cute musings, courtesy of three silly dogs—or, worse, one delusional man. If that is the case, then the fault lies not at their paws but squarely at my feet. Are my dogs fun and frustrating and loving and strange and wonderful? Yes. That is what dogs are. But I didn't want what they had to offer me and potentially others to get lost in all of the barking and the pooping and the licking and the treats, all of the typical stuff that comes with writing a book such as this. I guess that is the answer to the question, isn't it? Why did I keep writing?

Because they were worth the effort.

My Dachshunds were worth every keystroke and rewrite. And, even though they will never know what they have come to mean to me, I wanted as many people as possible to know about it. They kept teaching—I kept writing.

As hard as it is to believe, given what you now know of me, Baxter, Maya, and Molly really have taught me to doubt myself less. They have taught me to notice how important the little things are. To expect more from myself and people in general. They taught me that answers are often in plain sight—you just need to look for them. They taught me to see clearer, feel deeper, value more, and hate less. They taught me how to become what I hope I am: A better person. Still deeply flawed, hopelessly impatient, overly sensitive, reliably pessimistic, unapologetically sarcastic, and regrettably moody. But, all in all, better. And, of course, they taught me to dream.

I suppose, in the end, that's what my journey and this book are all about.

I suppose, in the end, that's the lowdown on life.

Afterword

Molly just turned four. On March 15, Maya will turn ten and formally enter her golden years. And Baxter, by turning six on May 2, will be embarking on the prime of his life, which for me translates to prime barking, prime begging, prime pooping, and prime staring—and as you know, that is what started this whole "life lessons" thing. As you also know by now, I wouldn't change a single thing about any of them: Baxter and his relentless pursuit of my insanity; Maya and her phobias; and Molly and her lethal licking.

I've heard it said that people don't necessarily get the dog they want but, rather, the dog they deserve. If that is the case, then I don't know what I did in this life, or even in a previous one, to deserve the dogs that are in my life...but it must not have been all that great.

Or I just might have been a saint.

They are a handful. And a hugful. Although at this point, it's probably a good time to tell you that after some considerable reflection, I've realized that what my dogs taught me aren't really life lessons at all. They're more like life reminders. I think that we've always had the capability within us to become better versions of ourselves. Maybe you even have instances of yourself doing just that. It's just that, well, life is annoyingly loud and overly messy and frustratingly complicated and busy and exhausting, and it's really easy to forget what each one of us can and should strive to be. I don't blame you for occasionally losing patience and forgetting to say "Thanks" and sometimes seeing only the bad in all things. Hey, line forms behind me! But it doesn't mean you and me and all of us should ever stop trying to be more than who we are. To be more than who we think we can be. And that's what I see in my wonderful Dachshunds. Black-and-tan and piebald reminders that I should keep at it. That I *do* have it in me, if not to succeed, then at least to *attempt* to succeed. We all have it in us. And who better to do the reminding than those who share their lives with us? Who see us at our best and our worst? And who give the very best of themselves to us? Who give their all to us?

I'm writing these words, quite literally, draped in Dachshunds. Baxter is lying between my legs, resting his muzzle on my ankle. Maya has my right arm pinned down, allowing just enough movement for me to type, but that's about it. And Molly is lying, based on a best guess, right above my heart. I'd really like to shed myself of their weight and get the blood circulating again in my extremities, but I don't dare move for fear of disturbing them. For today, at this moment, I want them to stay right where they are, because I know there will be a day that looks just like this one, when there will no longer be a great weight on my leg, I will have free and full movement of my right arm, and my heart will not feel as full and warm as it does right now. I want my friends to stay.

Besides, I still have much to learn.

Baxter is turning around. It's a bit like watching a turtle try to pivot on a dime. Okay, he did it. He is now facing me. He exhales loudly.

And begins, once again, to stare.

You'll have to excuse me: class is in session.

AMERICAN KENNEL CLUB®

Advocating for the purebred dog as a family companion, advancing canine health and well-being, working to protect the rights of all dog owners and promoting responsible dog ownership, the **American Kennel Club:**

Sponsors more than **22,000 sanctioned events** annually including conformation, agility, obedience, rally, tracking, lure coursing, earthdog, herding, field trial, hunt test, and coonhound events

Features a **10-step Canine Good Citizen® program** that rewards dogs who have good manners at home and in the community

Has reunited more than **370,000** lost pets with their owners through the AKC Companion Animal Recovery - visit **www.akccar.org**

Created and supports the AKC Canine Health Foundation, which funds research projects using the more than **$22 million** the AKC has donated since 1995 - visit **www.caninehealthfoundation.org**

Joins **animal lovers** through education, outreach and grant-making via the AKC Humane Fund - visit **www.akchumanefund.org**

We're more than champion dogs. We're the dog's champion.

www.akc.org